Lecture Notes in Computer Sci T0238104

Commenced Publication in 1973
Founding and Former Series Editors:
Gerhard Goos, Juris Hartmanis, and Jan van Leeuwen

Dirk Draheim   Gerald Weber (Eds.)

Trends in Enterprise Application Architecture

VLDB Workshop, TEAA 2005
Trondheim, Norway, August 28, 2005
Revised Selected Papers

 Springer

Volume Editors

Dirk Draheim
Freie Universität Berlin
Institute of Computer Science
Takustr. 9, 14195 Berlin, Germany
E-mail: draheim@acm.org

Gerald Weber
The University of Auckland
Department of Computer Science
38 Princes Street, Auckland 1020, New Zealand
E-mail: g.weber@cs.auckland.ac.nz

Library of Congress Control Number: 2006921983

CR Subject Classification (1998): H.2, H.4, C.2, H.3, J.1, K.4.4, I.2.11

LNCS Sublibrary: SL 3 – Information Systems and Application, incl. Internet/Web
and HCI

ISSN   0302-9743
ISBN-10   3-540-32734-7 Springer Berlin Heidelberg New York
ISBN-13   978-3-540-32734-9 Springer Berlin Heidelberg New York

Springer is a part of Springer Science+Business Media

springer.com

© Springer-Verlag Berlin Heidelberg 2006
Printed in Germany

Typesetting: Camera-ready by author, data conversion by Scientific Publishing Services, Chennai, India
Printed on acid-free paper   SPIN: 11681885   06/3142   5 4 3 2 1 0

Preface

TEAA 2005 (Trends in Enterprise Application Architecture) took place as a workshop of the conference VLDB 2005 (31st International Conference on Very Large Databases) in August 2005 in Trondheim, Norway.

Enterprise applications are mission critical for organizations. Currently there are several initiatives that see enterprise application integration as their natural playground, like Model Driven Architecture and Service Oriented Architecture. Now is the time to investigate how these approaches can provide added value. At TEAA 2005 the contributions identified a problem or issue in enterprise application architecture and proposed and evaluated a solution. The workshop benefited from lively discussions among the participants.

Applications, operating systems, database systems, hardware architecture and system administration concepts must be orchestrated to yield an optimized system architecture that tackles performance, stability, security, maintainability, and total cost of ownership. In practice, it is always a holistic view that is needed – it is known that system design approaches that overemphasize one of the software or hardware architecture aspects are likely to fail. In the TEAA 2005 workshop we examined the conceptual underpinnings of enterprise application architecture.

We are grateful to our keynote speaker Laura Haas for sharing her insights with us.

November 2005   Dirk Draheim
                                                                       Gerald Weber

Organization

Program Committee Chairs

Dirk Draheim   Freie Universität Berlin, Germany
Gerald Weber   University of Auckland, New Zealand

Program Committee

Ilkay Altintas	University of California, San Diego, USA
Thomas Arts	IT University of Göteborg, Sweden
Rajendra Bose	University of Edinburgh, UK
Mark van den Brand	Hogeschool van Amsterdam, Netherlands
Judith Cushing	The Evergreen State College, USA
Gill Dobbie	University of Auckland, New Zealand
Barry Dowdeswell	AARN Innovation Limited, New Zealand
Hannes Federrath	Universität Regensburg, Germany
James Frew	University of California, Santa Barbara, USA
Martin Große-Rhode	Fraunhofer ISST, Germany
Richard Hall	Laboratoire LSR-IMAG, France
Christoph Hartwich	Stamford Consultants, Switzerland
Josva Kleist	Aalborg University, Denmark
Christof Lutteroth	University of Auckland, New Zealand
Teresa Mallardo	Università degli Studi di Bari, Italy
Frank Maurer	University of Calgary, Canada
Josephine Micallef	Telcordia Technologies Inc., USA
Jan Newmarch	Monash University, Australia
Uday Reddy	University of Birmingham, UK
Wolfgang Rother	IBM Deutschland, Germany
Narendra Shivaji Chaudhari	Nanyang Technological University, Singapore
Marcin Sikorski	Gdansk University of Technology, Poland
Gerd Wagner	Universität Cottbus, Germany
Rajeev Wankar	University of Hyderabad, India
Yanchun Zhang	Victoria University, Australia

Table of Contents

Building an Information Infrastructure for Enterprise Applications

Laura Haas

IBM Silicon Valley Laboratory

In a modern enterprise, it is inevitable that different portions of the organization will use different systems to produce, store and search their critical data. Competition, evolving technology, mergers, acquisitions, and geographic distribution all contribute to this diversity. Only by combining these various systems can the enterprise realize the full value of the data they contain. Yet building new applications across these various information sources can be amazingly painful, forcing developers to discover what data is where, figure out what it means, and learn myriad different interfaces.

An information infrastructure to address this challenge must offer users access to any data in the enterprise and the means of reaching additional data external to the enterprise, from partners, suppliers, etc. The infrastructure should provide appropriate integration technologies to support, alone or in combination, important enterprise usage patterns. It should connect islands of data into a single virtual information source, so that application development is vastly simplified.

To motivate this vision, this talk explores several real-life enterprise application challenges and the information technology needed to support them. It presents currently available technology building blocks, and identifies some future challenges in building a strategic information infrastructure for enterprise applications.

D. Draheim and G. Weber (Eds.): TEAA 2005, LNCS 3888, p. 1, 2006.
© Springer-Verlag Berlin Heidelberg 2006

Evaluating Integration Architectures – A Scenario-Based Evaluation of Integration Technologies

Stephan Aier and Marten Schönherr

Technische Universität Berlin, Sekr. FR 6-7, Franklinstr. 28/29, 10587 Berlin
stephan.aier@tu-berlin.de, mschoenherr@sysedv.tu-berlin.de
http://www.sysedv.tu-berlin.de/eai

Abstract. A major aspect of complex Enterprise Architectures is the integration of existing heterogeneous IT-systems in a business process oriented way. The paper starts with the definition of terms as Enterprise Architecture and process orientation. Based on an empirical study the paper shows that there is no significant business process orientation in information system integration projects. Among other reasons this is due to deficits in understanding and managing integration methods and technologies. Therefore the paper addresses the evaluation and comparison of relevant integration architectures as a first step to work on that issue. The paper differentiates individually coded interfaces, centralized hub&spoke and distributed approaches based on standardized interface descriptions (Service Oriented Architecture – SOA). The mentioned empirical study was extended by an action research based prototyping to assure a reliable evaluation and comparison of the three integration architectures. To make them comparable they have been implemented in the same fictitious business scenario which is described briefly. The paper finally compares the integration architectures with a set of 11 criteria which summarize over 400 variables taken into consideration in the evaluation process. The conclusion of the paper is not a solution but a suggestion for further research.

1 Enterprise Architecture – Harmonizing Business Processes and IT Architecture Using Integration Concepts

In the current discussion on integrative enterprise architectures generic approaches are missing – an industry standard is far away. A precondition for the standardization of methods and technologies is the definition of generally accepted requirements and criteria. A common understanding of criteria supports or even enables an evaluation of the appropriateness of both: methods and technologies of integration concepts.

The paper starts with foundations concerning methodological and technological aspects of integrative enterprise architectures followed by a 3 step approach which includes an empirical study on the understanding and use of integration

D. Draheim and G. Weber (Eds.): TEAA 2005, LNCS 3888, pp. 2–14, 2006.

concepts, a prototypical implementation of different integration architectures and finally the evaluation of the chosen integration architectures based on the study and the implementation. The 11 criteria used for the evaluation were taken from an industry funded survey which used more than 400 variables to evaluate integration technology sets including middleware and EAI (Enterprise Application Integration). Considering length restrictions the paper will briefly introduce the chosen integration architectures along the 11 criteria. Two criteria will be described in detail.

An important precondition for a stringent consideration is a coherent understanding of *enterprise architecture*. An architecture can be understood as an abstract, holistic view on structures and patterns [1]. Architectures are usually the result of a planning process and thus represent a master plan for holistic realization of future measures. These general characteristics applied on enterprises lead to the term of enterprise architectures. Enterprise architecture is the combination of organizational, technical, and psychosocial aspects during planning and development of socio-technical business information systems. The paper addresses organizational and technical aspects of enterprise architectures. Therefore we use the terms organizational architecture and IT architecture. Our understanding uses the term integration concept which refers to methods and technologies supporting the integration of information systems in a business process oriented way. In this context the term business process is not following a consistently accepted definition. In our understanding a business process is the sequence of at least two activities which are based on tasks relevant in a business context done by employees responsible for the execution and/or control of the activity or task. Especially in the context of the paper a business process has to be distinguished from technical processes which are describing technical activities or tasks as messaging, exception handling or similar concepts executed by IT infrastructures not human beings (Fig. 1).

Organizational architecture contains all non-technical components. It is similar to the instrumental understanding of an organization which includes all explicit regulations for structures and processes. We differentiate organizational architecture into organizational structure and business processes. IT architecture stands complementary to organizational architecture. It covers all technical

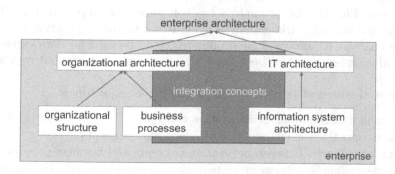

Fig. 1. Enterprise Architecture

components of enterprise architectures - especially information systems with their individual information system architecture.

In scientific literature the terms organizational architecture and IT architecture are used inconsistently. Depending on the authors background organizational architecture addresses technical aspects [2] and IT architecture contains organizational issues [3]. We keep the concepts separated to emphasize their importance. This seems to make sense, since there are complex interdependencies between both of them and they significantly influence operational efficiency of enterprises [4, 5, 6, 7, 8].

Due to changing business requirements business processes usually need to be changed frequently. The IT architecture has to meet the new requirements in an efficient way. Complex, historically grown and therefore heterogeneous IT infrastructures are not designed in a manner which would support changing requirements. The ability of supporting changing requirements is described as sustainability of enterprise architectures [8]. Integration concepts are a possible solution to increase sustainability of enterprise architectures hence reconcile organizational and IT architecture in an agile and volatile surrounding.

The field of sustainable enterprise architecture suffers from a lack of academic, empiric and generic approaches. Therefore we made a study on integration concepts in the context of enterprise architecture which is described in the next chapters.

2 Empirical Study – Objectives and Method

The study analyses how large organizations implement and use system integration concepts focusing on technology and their interdependencies to organizational aspects hence structures and business processes. These research issues have been analyzed in a descriptive and explorative manner. The study has been designed as a non-experimental cross section enquiry over a short period of time primarily using a written standardized questionnaire. Based on the results of the predominant descriptive and quantitative analysis a second questioning has been made. It was based on expert interviews hold individually or in small groups. The purpose of this evaluation was to verify the results and a possibly underlying thesis. Finally a factor analysis has completed the empirical study. Using 14 variables this multivariate analysis generated 4 factors supporting the quantitative analysis. 63 answered questionnaires could be used for data extraction. 5 individual interviews had been done and 25 people participated in a group workshop.

The study categorizes results in the following 4 major topics:

- common understanding of integration concepts
- how to organize the introduction of integration concepts
- interdependencies between integration concepts and business processes
- interdependencies between integration concepts and organizational structures

The next chapter will describe a compendium of the first and the third aspect only due to their relevance for the context of the paper.

3 Integration Concepts – Common Understanding and Interdependencies with Business Processes

Integration concepts are generally understood as an established technology predominantly used in large organizations to implement connectivity between existing IS and to replace individually coded interfaces. It is considered to be a strategic long-term element of IT architecture providing a modular toolset basically including software adapters (connectors), data transformation tools (mapping), monitoring and workflow features and business process management functionality. To operate implemented integration infrastructure even huge organizations employ a few technically well educated staff members only. Compared to the immense effort accepted during the implementation phase it is surprising that just a few people are carrying the valuable knowledge according to a very expensive infrastructural investment hence many organizations do not pay as much attention as necessary to an integrated understanding of the enterprise architecture. Even if the responsibility for integration infrastructures is located in a department responsible for organizational development issues usually there are too few people to manage the challenge. Furthermore the common understanding of integration concepts is technology driven hence in many cases the IT department operates integration infrastructures. IT departments usually provide enough manpower but not the organizational understanding of business processes nor the authority to influence organizational issues. Therefore the IT department is not the right instance to be responsible for architectural issues in the manner of a holistic conception.

The objective to design and run Integration Concepts in a business process oriented fashion has rarely been reached in practice. Implementations done in a process oriented way usually mean technical processes as e.g. message queuing and exception handling not business processes (Fig. 2).

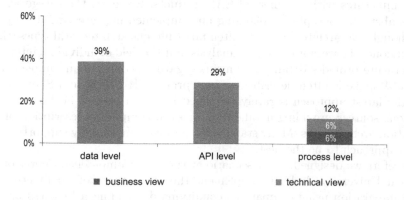

Fig. 2. Process Orientation in Integration Projects

However, in most cases integration projects cause business process changes. These projects shall lead to better, more efficient and faster business processes. The most important process changes are automation and consolidation. These process adaptations result in more formalization of organizational structures. Hence integration approaches are indirect enablers for business processes which only become feasible through such projects.

As a result of the empirical study there are no significant implementations in the companies questioned reconciling business processes and IT architecture in the meaning of a holistic enterprise architecture due to the dominance of a technology driven understanding of integration concepts. The methodological aspect in Integration Concepts mentioned above is not taken into consideration on a sufficient level. This result has motivated further considerations described in the next chapters.

4   Methodology vs. Technology

Integration projects with the objective of harmonizing organizational and IT architecture usually deal with non-technical issues too. Irrespective from the integration topic reflections on methodological and technical aspects have a long tradition in the research on information systems.

After studying the relevant literature we state that holistic architectural concepts consist of interrelated methodological and technical aspects. Methods and Methodologies can be found amongst others in the filed of Enterprise Architecture Frameworks [9, 10] and in the approaches of organizational and technical patterns of integrated architectural design [11, 12, 13].

The paper focuses in a first approach on evaluation criteria of relevant integration architectures. Literature on integration technologies often uses product related categorizations [14, 15]. The present article uses three categories based on the architecture of the integration solution itself. We differentiate between individually coded unidirectional or bidirectional point-to-point interfaces, centralized hub&spoke architectures, and decentralized service oriented architectures (SOA). To some extend it is possible to implement these categories of integration architectures with commercial EAI products. However, the categories are used as abstract concepts for planning and implementing integration projects. Even though real architectures will often mix different architectural types, these abstract concepts are suitable for an analysis. For the field of individual interfaces [18] literature provides detailed comments regarding concepts and implementation, hub&spoke is often described as best practice [14, 15, 8] and SOA [16, 17] being the latest approach is rarely described in literature yet. So far there are no serious sources providing a validation or even comparing description of the integration architectures. Many statements are even emotionally supporting one specific approach to be the best.

Therefore we designed a test scenario at the EAI Competence Center of the Technical University Berlin to implement the three types of architecture for system integration using comparable conditions demanding a business process oriented implementation.

The general facts according to the test scenario and the implementation of the three integration architectures in the test scenario will be described briefly in the next chapter. A detailed description would not fit the length restriction of the paper.

5 Scenario

The fictitious medium-sized company WMYPC (We Make Your PC) sells customized computer systems starting from small multimedia computers to enterprise server systems. The company consists of five departments. The business processes of all departments are modeled using UML activity diagrams. These processes are supported by six individually implemented information systems and one off the shelf software product. Hence the firms IT landscape is heterogeneous. The seven existing information systems use three different concepts of data storage and are distributed over several computers. The aim of the test scenario was to realize an adequately complex business environment with business processes selectively supported by heterogeneous information systems.

After business process definition, modeling and implementation of the scenario's IT infrastructure we have integrated the existing information systems in a business process oriented way with the described architectural types each in an own scenario.

Uni- and bidirectional interfaces have been implemented on the basis of XML documents which are exchanged manually (batch). The hub&spoke implementation has been done on seven commercial EAI products. For process orientation

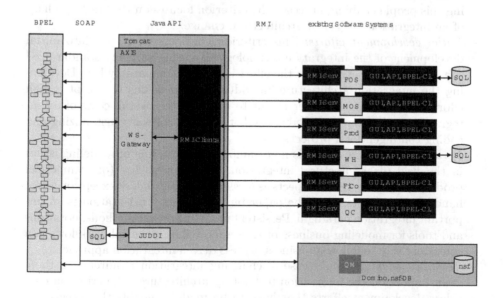

Fig. 3. Integration Architecture SOA

we have used and evaluated the modeling components provided by the respective tool vendors. The SOA has been implemented using web services technology. Orchestration has been done with ORACLE BPEL Manager and BPEL4WS. The seven information systems are encapsulated in 58 services and executed with four BPEL processes. Figure 3 shows the SOA integration architecture. The scenario – business processes as well as IT architecture – are the same for all three architectural implementations.

The following chapter briefly describes 11 criteria used for the evaluation and comparison of the integration architectures implemented. They have been created by merging over 400 detailed variables used in an industrial project surveying integration technologies. The evaluation and comparison uses results from the empirical study and experiences from the prototypical implementation considering the 400 variables. Still the presented results are not generic in the sense of being universally valid in any situation. They have to be taken as a basis for further research.

6   Criteria and Evaluation

To evaluate and compare the integration architectures we used the following criteria considering numerous detailed aspects according to design time and run time characteristics of the implemented architectures.

- *Initial planning efforts:* Implying an existing IT department, the criterion considers efforts needed to support internal staff with the ability/competence/knowledge to design, implement and run the integration technology and/or the costs of mandating external consultancy for supporting this people enabling process. The criterion focuses on the starting phase of an integration project or architectural change.
- *Initial development efforts:* This criterion considers effort put into initial development of the integration technology. By using as many standardized software products as possible the effort is usually comparably low. Developing the integration architecture individually often means to accept a high effort. The criterion is rather meant to evaluate the overall costs of an integration project but to differentiate between the software customizing and coding contingent of a project.
- *Persistent modeling:* There is no common understanding of modeling issues in the field of architectural integration. Most approaches (or commercial products) model technical aspects as message queuing and/or exception/error handling etc. As stated in the paper business process orientation is an important integration paradigm. Persistent modeling means methods, notations and tools for modeling business processes as well as technical workflows in a consistent way to follow a business process driven integration approach.
- *Technical adaptations:* In case of changing integration requirements there is an impact on the integration technology architecture. The criterion considers development efforts that have to be made to enable the integration architecture to meet new requirements.

- *Non-invasive legacy/host integration:* Particularly monolithic coded software systems without standardized interface descriptions or even connectors are very hard to integrate in enterprise architectures. Many organizations running legacy systems are not going to change these systems to improve their adaptability due to reasons of stability, complexity and the risk which comes with a system change. This criterion describes the ability of the considered integration architectures to integrate so called legacy systems in a non-invasive way.
- *Security:* Integrating complex enterprise architectures is even more a security issue than considering security aspects of a single software system. Integration is driven by system communication and multi-user impact. Therefore this criterion evaluates the integration architectures according to their security features. This criterion becomes even more important considering cross-company processes.
- *Maintainability:* The criterion compares features (general administration tools, load balancing, meta data management, monitoring etc.) and efforts to maintain an integration architecture.
- *Customizability:* Customizing integration architectures to meet changing requirements seems to be the complement to 'technical adaptations'. However, there are many situations where changes do not need to affect the technical structure of integration architectures but ask for a specific degree of freedom in customizing existing features according to the requirements. Usually generic elements as customizable objects, adapters or even generic front end forms increase the degree of customizability.
- *Stability:* This criterion considers the technical reliability of integration architectures. Failover or offline state is needed to be minimized in complex enterprise architectures due to direct and indirect impact on secondary areas as data and business process quality and processing time.
- *Transactionality:* Transacting huge amounts of data in a specific time is one of the common tasks in software system communication and integration. Transactionality guarantees a complete processing of a specific number of interactions between information systems as a single coherent step, i. e. either all interactions will be processed or not. This may include a rollback of interactions. This criterion becomes crucial and demanding at the same time with complex business processes distributed among several information systems.
- *Costs of operation:* Operating integration architectures addresses a significant quota of the overall costs. They should be taken into consideration when choosing the right integration architecture.

Table 1 summarizes the results of the evaluation and comparison process. Due to the fact that the results are partly depending on experimental research design the chosen scale seams to be crude but sufficient and adequate for the objective.

The evaluation and especially the comparison have to be interpreted in direct relation between the different architectures. For example a 'very poor' demonstrates a characteristic compared with the other evaluated architectures not an absolute evaluation.

Table 1. Evaluation of integration architectures: −− very poor, − poor, ○ neutral, + good, ++ very good

criteria	individual interfaces	hub& spoke	SOA
initial planning efforts	+	−−	−
initial development efforts	−	+	−
persistent modeling	−	++	+
technical adaptations	+	○	+
non-invasive legacy/host integration	−−	+	○
security	++	+	−
maintainability	−−	++	−
customizability	−−	++	−
stability	++	+	○
transactionality	++	○	−
costs of operation	−−	+	○

Due to lenght restrictions we will explain which arguments led to the respective evaluation of the alternative architectures for two of the criteria only – initial planning efforts and persistent modeling.

Initial planning efforts for designing and planning the implementation of an individually coded point-to-point interface are often quite moderate especially when information systems provide documented interface descriptions. A necessary precondition is existing basic know-how in the integration technologies applied – usually widespread programming languages. This is true for most IT departments of large companies.

In comparison there is often no significant competence for complex EAI integration tools (hub&spoke) which not only aim at the connection of two information systems but on the integration of a whole IT/IS landscape. Such projects are not only technologically demanding but also methodologically because the project has to consider many different requirements and stakeholder interests. As the empiric study points out this usually causes a massive involvement of external consultancy. Figure 4 shows that most integration projects make use of external consultancy in the fields of project management, technical support, IT architecture etc. hence the initial planning efforts are immense compared to the implementation of an individual interface. Prototyping the EAI hub&spoke architectures in the test scenario has been very demanding especially in the first phases when it came to the understanding of proprietary technologies, methods and features offered by different EAI vendors. Once understood the implementation was fast and efficient.

Initial planning efforts implementing an SOA is methodologically as demanding as the hub & spoke architecture especially because there are neither formal guidelines nor many best practices in the field of designing SOA. Technologically it is less demanding due to standardized straightforward technologies used in SOA such as web service descriptions. The use of standards in SOA compared to many proprietary features in EAI (hub&spoke) reduces initial planning

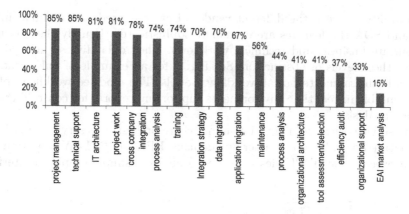

Fig. 4. Frequencies of external consultancy services in EAI projects

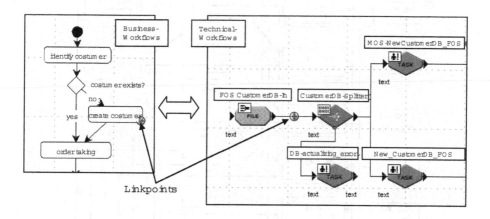

Fig. 5. Connecting business and technical workflow models in EAI

efforts. The effort is much higher compared to an individual interface especially because *Persistent modeling* is rated poor for individually coded interfaces due to the fact that individual interfaces are usually implemented not according to generic business process requirements but individual requirements of connectivity, transactionality and syntactical mappings considering the specific software systems. There is no generic or standardized modeling approach, method, notation or tool used to design and implement individual interfaces considering business processes used in practice. Some might use modeling techniques to support the implementation of individually coded interfaces but the empirical study found out that hub&spoke or SOA replace point to point interfaces for reasons of more generic modeling features offered by these architectures.

EAI (hub&spoke) has been evaluated as 'very good' in the criterion of persistent modeling. All implemented products offer modeling methods, notations and tools with graphical user interfaces. There are definitely differences in quality and usability between the different vendors but compared to individual interfaces and SOA the features are extremely sophisticated. Usually the products differentiate business and technical workflows. They offer diverse methods to connect these levels of abstraction. See Fig. 5 for an example of link points to connect business and technical workflow models. The modeled workflows often are executable in real time environments supporting reports for controlling and business analysis.

The service oriented integration architecture orchestrates services in a basic or structured way. To do so a script language BPEL (BPEL4WS) and an engine to execute the BPEL files is needed. Usually a simple graphical interface

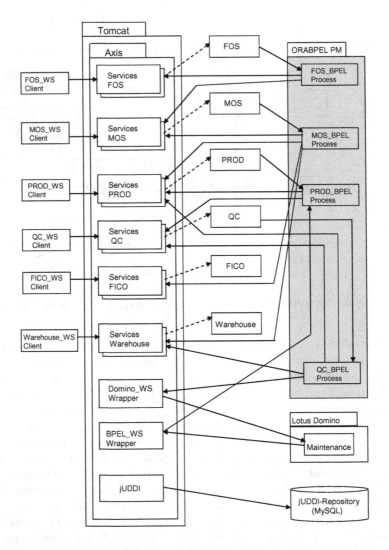

Fig. 6. Encapsulated and orchestrated services in a SOA

is provided to model the service composition. There is a huge variety in orchestrating services especially structures as sequences, parallel flows, switches, loops and event driven activities. Often the graphical interface is not featuring all possible modeling algorithms therefore a development environment to implement script languages is provided. Programming competence is essential for this kind of modeling. A composition of simple services to complex services is possible. The SOA has been evaluated as 'good' in the criterion of persistent modeling due to fact that there is a possibility of orchestrating and composing services along business processes using standardized references and tools. Still there are deficits in usability and full execution of complex business processes by modeled services. There is a high potential but the approach will need some more time to become approved. An important unsolved issue is the granularity used in the service definition phase. Without generic service definition rules there is no structured way to a later orchestration of services according to business process requirements due to the fact that flexible orchestration heavily depends on the technical implementation of a service. The implemented SOA encapsulates 58 services used and orchestrated in four BPEL processes. See Fig. 6 for an overview.

Web services are just one way to implement SOA. Therefore BPEL is not an overall standard for modeling services. The approaches used in modeling SOA are mostly based on UML and BPEL and focused on technological details. A stringent persistent modeling between business and technical processes depends on the specific implementation. The described deficits lead to an evaluation of 'good' especially according to the mentioned future potential.

7 Conclusion

Integration concepts as a central approach to sustainability in enterprise architectures need appropriate methods and technologies. There are few generic approaches guiding the practitioner towards a sustainable enterprise architecture. The paper delivers first results on surveying interdependencies between relevant parts of an enterprise architecture and on evaluating different architectures to integrate the interrelated architectural elements (business processes and IT architecture). After evaluating and comparing integration architectures there are no generic patterns which could be used to suggest a single architectural approach to be the most appropriate integration architecture in general. Specific situational requirements guide to the right technology mix used for an integration concept. As a result of the empirical study described in the paper there is a lack of holistic architectural understanding. Methods need to be developed considering life cycle aspects in persistent modeling. A stringent modeling approach containing a methodology, methods and notations should be developed. Modeling different levels (from business to technical processes) and taking time line issues of the mentioned architectural elements into account are just first ideas for further work on methodical aspects of enterprise architecture.

References

1. Bass, L., Clements, P., Kazman, R.: Software Architecture in Practice. 2nd ed., Pearson Education Inc., Boston (2003)
2. Nadler, D.A., Gerstein, M.S., Shaw, R.B.: Organizational architecture – designs for changing organizations. Jossey-Bass, San Francisco (1992)
3. Zachmann, J.A.: A Framework for Information Systems Architecture. In: IBM Systems Journal **26** (1987) pp. 276–292
4. Markus, M., Robey, D.: Information technology and organizational change: Causal structure in theory and research. Management Science **34** (1988) S. 583–589
5. Leavitt, H., Whisler, T.: Management in the 1980s: New information flows cut new organization flows. Harvard Business Review **36** (1958) S. 41–48
6. Lewin, A.Y., Hunter, S.D.: Information Technology & Organizational Design: A Longitudinal Study of Information Technology Implementations in the U.S. Retailing Industrie, 1980-1996. In: H. Glaser, E.F. Schröder, A. v. Werder, (eds.) Organisation im Wandel der Märkte. Gabler, Wiesbaden (1998) S. 251–286
7. Venkatraman, N.V.: IT-Induced Business Reconfiguration. In: Scott Morton, M.S. (ed.) The Corporation of the 1990s. Information Technology and Organizational Transformation. Oxford University Press, New York (1991) pp. 122–158
8. Aier, S.: Sustainability of Enterprise Architecture and EAI. Soliman, K.S. (ed.) Information Technology and Organizations in the 21st Century: Challenges & Solutions. Proceedings of The 2004 International Business Information Management Conference, International Business Information Management Association (IBIMA), Amman, Jordan, (2004), pp. 182–189.
9. Schekkerman, J.: How to survive in the Jungle of Enterprise Architecture Frameworks. Trafford, Victoria, Canada (2004)
10. Noran, O.S.: A Mapping of Individual Architecture Frameworks onto GERAM. In: Bernus, P., Nemes, L., Schmidt, G. (Ed.) Handbook on Enterprise Architecture. Springer, Berlin (2003) pp. 65–212
11. Fowler, M. (ed.): Patterns of Enterprise Application Architecture. MITP, Boston (2003)
12. Hohpe, G., Woolf, B.: Enterprise Integration Patterns. Addison-Wesley, Boston (2004)
13. Brown, W.J., Malveau, R.C., McCormick, H.W., et al.: Anti Patterns. mitp, Bonn (2004)
14. Linthicum, D.S.: Enterprise Application Integration. Addison-Wesley Longman, Amsterdam (2000)
15. Ruh, W.A., Maginnis, F.X., Brown, W.J.: Enterprise Application Integration. Wiley, John, & Sons, New York (2001)
16. Krafzig, D., Banke, K., Slama, D.: Enterprise SOA: Service-Oriented Architecture. Prentice Hall, Upper Saddle River, NJ (2005)
17. Erl, T.: Service-oriented architecture: A Field Guide to integrating XML and Web Services. Prentice Hall, Upper Saddle River, NJ (2004)
18. Juric, M.B., Basha, S.J., Leander, R., et al.: Professional J2EE EAI. wrox, Birmingham (2001)

Integrating a Software Product Line with Rule-Based Business Process Modeling

N. Ilker Altintas[1] and Semih Cetin[2]

[1] Cybersoft Information Technologies Co., Atasehir Bulvari, Ata Plaza 3/3, 34758,
Atasehir, Istanbul - Turkey
ilker.altintas@cs.com.tr
[2] Cybersoft Information Technologies Co., Silikon Blok, No:18, 06531,
ODTU Teknokent, Ankara - Turkey
semih.cetin@cs.com.tr

Abstract. This paper proposes an approach to integrate a software product line (Aurora) with reflective rule-based business process modeling (RUMBA). Aurora is a service-oriented application development and execution platform supporting today's well known "Rich Internet Applications" and "Enterprise Internet Applications" concepts. On the other hand, RUMBA is a rule-based model in which rules and rule-sets can be expressed in terms of dynamic aspects and delegated facts. The proposed approach mainly addresses "Reflective Aspect" and "Reflective Rule" patterns for the seamless integration of Aurora and RUMBA. Both architectural patterns introduce a "generative" approach for developing the basic aspects, dynamic rules and rule-sets so that all can be implemented in the Adaptive Object Model (AOM). The proposed model will be explained in detail and exemplified with existing projects using both Aurora and RUMBA approaches.

1 Introduction

Effective management of business processes executed in evolving software infrastructures becomes more and more important today. Thus, responding to ever changing business requirements in shorter cycles may put an organization ahead of others in the stiff competition. One simple way to achieve business responsiveness is speeding up the software development process with advanced reusability techniques provided by Software Product Lines (SPL) [5]. Another might be the separation of concerns for "core business logic" and "business rules" where core business logic can be implemented by IT departments whereas business rules can be defined and managed by business departments along with the administrative tools again provided by IT departments.

Most of the organizations neither employ SPL approach nor the separation of concerns for core business logic and business rules. Even if they do rarely, they don't have an intention to use both at the same time for a more capable SPL and/or better business process modeling. This paper will propose an approach to integrate an SPL (called as Aurora) with reflective rule-based business process modeling (called as RUMBA). Aurora is a service-oriented application development and execution platform even supporting today's well known Rich Internet Applications (RIA) and

D. Draheim and G. Weber (Eds.): TEAA 2005, LNCS 3888, pp. 15–28, 2006.

Enterprise Internet Applications (EIA) concepts [28,29,30]. On the other hand, RUMBA (Rule-Based Model for Basic Aspects) is the rule-based business process modeling approach implemented with aspect-oriented techniques.

The approach mainly proposes two architectural patterns for the seamless integration of Aurora and RUMBA: "Reflective Aspect Pattern" and "Reflective Rule Pattern". Both patterns are using a "generative" approach for the implementation of basic aspects, rules and rule-sets in the Adaptive Object Model (AOM) [19,20]. In order not to keep this approach only at conceptual level, contribution of the study will be exemplified at every suitable point on existing architectural model of Aurora and developing rule-based model of RUMBA. Both approaches have been employed in several enterprise scale projects ranging from core banking to insurance. These projects will be introduced very briefly as well to emphasize the software quality factors achieved by using the approach.

2 Aurora Software Product Line

An SPL is a set of software-intensive systems sharing a common, managed set of features that satisfies the specific needs of a particular market segment or mission and that are developed from a common set of core assets in a prescribed way. A product line's scope is a description of the products constituting the product line or what the product line is capable of producing [5].

Aurora is a platform independent SPL including core infrastructure based on RIA and EIA concepts for enterprise Web applications plus the software process management methodology, WYSIWYG (What You See Is What You Get) design and development environments, configuration management techniques and tools. In order to eliminate the avoidable coding efforts throughout the software development lifecycle, Aurora provides techniques and tools for every tier of Web application development.

The Aurora product line has been constructed on the common architectural models of various enterprise systems such as core banking, tax collection, insurance and central registry authority. Hence, with the disciplined reuse of core assets and commonalities it can address the generic problems of performance, cost reduction, complexity management, maintenance of too many product variants, and responsiveness to customer/marketplace demands.

As Zubrow and Chastek stated [4], the key component enabling effective resolution of these problems is the use of a product line architecture that allows an organization to identify and reuse software artifacts for the efficient creation of products sharing some commonality, but varying in known and managed ways. The architecture, in a sense, is the glue that holds the product line together. Therefore, before addressing the proposed approach for that with reflective aspects and rules, the following subsections will briefly describe the multi-tier architecture of Aurora (depicted in Fig. 1) and the associated software process management methodology.

In [4], study of measurement criteria for software product lines indicated two major sets: measurement for SPL management and measures for asset development management. However the discussion is beyond the scope of this paper and explained in another paper entitled by "Aurora Software Product Line" which addresses the organizational and methodological issues as well [6].

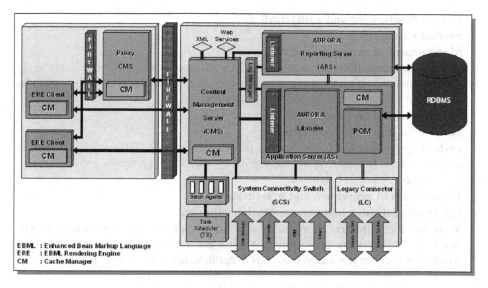

Fig. 1. Multi-tier Architecture of the Aurora Infrastructure

2.1 Presentation Tier

As a reflex to the limitations of HTML, RIA concept introduced the client-side rendering approach that can present very dense, responsive, and graphically rich user interfaces [28,29,30]. It combines best of the desktop, Web, and communications [3]. In parallel to the basic targets of RIA, the Aurora presentation tier has been designed with "Zero Development and Deployment Model (ZDDM)" for building rich clients without compromising the ultra-thin deployment model. Moreover, the Aurora presentation tier does not address only rendering screens but also reporting and printing capabilities together with client side dynamic caching.

The Aurora presentation tier has been derived from User Interface Markup Language (UIML) [1], which is an open standard user interface description language in XML that can be freely implemented by anyone. The motivation of UIML is to facilitate better tools for creation of user interfaces that work on any platform available today, but which also will allow today's legacy user interfaces to evolve to new forms for use on new platforms.

2.2 Content Management Tier

The Aurora content management tier acts like a bridge from the presentation tier to the application tier. Content Management Server (CMS) which is the heart of the Aurora architectural design, provides the following capabilities:

- **Separation of layout from actual data:** EBML provides its designers to specify screen layout and behavior in terms of event-handling and rule management. However, the transactional data is completely isolated from them and handled separately using remote calls. CMS maps the remote call requests coming from clients and external systems to the component services hosted by the J2EE application servers. As a result, EBML screen layouts and behaviors can be cached separately.

- **User authentication and authorization.**
- **Session management.**
- **Management of session state data.**
- **Client communication management:** CMS can communicate to the clients using different policies in terms of compression and encryption. Different policies can be applied on varying IPs, roles and user properties.
- **Management of client cacheable objects.**
- **Load balancing and Web switching.**
- **Instant query presentation:** Aurora provides advanced GUI controls to search reference data. Instant requests are replied by CMS, query results are cached and served page-by-page on demand.
- **Report content generation and presentation.**
- **Internationalization and personalization support.**
- **Web Services support:** Every core service in Aurora can be deployed as Web Services without any extra line-of-code. WSDLs are automatically generated from the Aurora core service repository, thus B2B integration is as simple as a "point & click".

2.3 Application Tier – Service-Oriented Architecture (SOA)

The Aurora application model provides a clear separation of business logic from the content management and data persistence. The component-based architecture results in partitioning the business logic into proper components (set of objects) in such a way both to maximize intra-component relations (coherency) and minimize inter-component interactions (coupling) [24,25]. The Aurora application tier and development tools both provide the optimum granularity to satisfy business requirements in an efficient way. The high-level organization and run-time execution model of the Aurora middle tier is fully compliant with SOA [21,22].

The Aurora application model uses a simple component object model divided into two categories: "Business Object Model (BOM)" and "Persistent Object Model (POM)". Service Executor (SE) is the global coordinator of services accessing BOM and POM, thus components are independent of each other to provide isolation and parallelism during both development and maintenance. Web services are not considered as the only mean of implementing SOA in Aurora, rather it is just one way of access to a service-based system [23].

2.4 Data Tier and Connectivity Model

The Aurora data tier usually consists of an XA compliant RDBMS on behalf of Java Transaction Server (JTS). It manipulates database requests through an implied O2R mapping layer. Moreover, the Aurora POM architecture can also help establish data connections with legacy applications through XA-compliant agents (see Fig. 2).

The component model can access POM classes defined by the application developers using Aurora POM Studio (GUI environment to manage POM). POM Studio can generate the needed scripts, associated DDL schema and related static Java classes automatically from these definitions. The O2R mapping tool of Aurora can map the stored procedures, functions, views and queries as well. In addition, other persistent object mapping frameworks, such as Hibernate [2], can also be plugged and used.

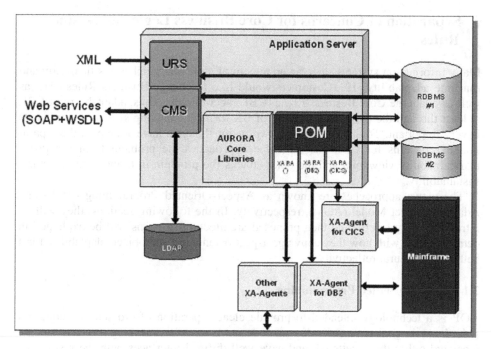

Fig. 2. Aurora Connectivity and Integration Technologies

For integration with other information systems including the legacy ones, a separate module, called as System Connectivity Switch (SCS), has been implemented. SCS provides the integration between application tier and existing source of information. The global transaction management also covering the legacy systems is carried out by SCS using the XA compliant agents needed by Java Connector Architecture (JCA). Fig. 2 shows the perspective of Aurora for Enterprise Application Integration (EAI) using XML and Web Services, transactional and non-transactional connectors and adaptors (see [26,27] for EAI).

2.5 Software Process Management Methodology

One of the most critical elements of SPL concept is the accompanied development and software process management methodology [5]. Aurora provides a methodology for complete software development life cycle ensuring the software development process to be well-defined, reusable and manageable. The methodology is built around a software process management repository, which organizes development processes and defines the roles and responsibilities of every team member.

Prototyping is another cornerstone of the design process in Aurora. The Aurora testing process defines the organization of test team, members' roles and responsibilities, scenario management, run management and issue tracking. Aurora also defines other issues such as requirement management, change management, quality management and documentation management. However, details of the methodology will not be discussed here due to page limitations.

3 Separation of Concerns for Core Business Logic and Business Rules

Many information systems share an architectural style that emphasizes flexibility and run-time adaptability [19]. Customers would like to change Business Rules (BR) as well as adapt the Core Business Logic (CBL) accordingly. Thus, adaptability of CBL at least through the dynamic flexibility of BR to meet changing system requirements is very important. To this end, at least two major thoughts have attempted the separation of concerns for CBL and BR. One approaches the problem from functional maintainability viewpoint and the other attacks the problem in terms of architectural sustainability.

These two approaches are known as Aspect-Oriented Programming (AOP) and Adaptive Object Model (AOM), respectively. In the following sections, they will be introduced very briefly and then proposed architectural patterns will be explained in detail together with how they converge aspect orientation and object adaptability for a better architectural reflectivity.

3.1 Aspect-Oriented Programming

AOP is a technology intended to provide clear separation of crosscutting concerns [14]. Its main goal is to make design, code more modular, meaning the concerns are localized rather than scattered, and have well-defined interfaces with the rest of the system. In this way, AOP solves the issues raised by some design decisions that are difficult to cleanly capture in code [17]. Those issues are called aspects, and AOP is intended to provide appropriate isolation, composition and reuse of the code used to implement them. Nowadays, several AOP approaches such as AspectJ, Composition Filters, HyperJ and DemeterJ are available [7,9,13,16,18].

AOP paradigm proposes that computer systems are better programmed by separately specifying the various concerns (properties or areas of interest), which are composed or weaved together into a coherent program [15]. This is especially useful when the concerns are crosscutting that correspond to design decisions, which involve several objects or operations leading to different places in the code that do the same thing, or do a coordinated simple thing. In addition to several examples of crosscutting concerns such as logging, distribution, persistence, security, authentication, performance, transactions integrity, as pointed out by D'Hont, AOP is a very good technique to be used in the separation of concerns for CBL and BR as well [11].

3.2 Adaptive Object Model

Architectures that are designed to adapt to new user requirements by retrieving descriptive information that can be interpreted at runtime are sometimes called as "reflective architectures" or "meta architectures". AOM architecture is based on a particular kind of reflective architecture. AOM is needed for business applications that manage products of some sort and are extended to add new products with the appropriate business rules [20].

AOM is a model that represents classes, attributes, and relationships as metadata. The system is a model based on instances rather than classes. Users change the metadata (object model) to reflect changes in the domain. These changes modify the system's behavior. In other words, it stores its object model in a database and interprets it. Consequently, the object model is active, when you change it, the system changes immediately. This is the reason why AOM can be classified as a reflective architecture. The AOM is good if the system is constantly changing or if you want to allow users to dynamically configure and extend their system. It can lead to a system that allows users to "program without programming" [19].

The design of AOM involves three major activities: defining the business entities, rules and relationships; developing a design of an engine for instantiating and manipulating these entities according to their rules in the application; and developing tools for describing these entities, rules and relationships [19,20,10]. To this end, AOM proposes various patterns to achieve these activities, but there is no generic framework for building them. Thus, reflectivity is an implied concept in AOM and the user should provide by itself a generic administration environment (a reflective middleware) to achieve that reflectivity. Additionally, separation of concerns in CBL and BR is not a first-level target in AOM but could be achieved by carefully employing appropriate architectural and/or design patterns.

3.3 Convergence of AOP and AOM: The Reflective Aspect Pattern

Adaptability or dynamism of software systems is not a new concern in software engineering. As introduced before, AOP and AOM have been proposed as full-fledged approaches to attack the problem of application adaptability or dynamism. However, it is our observation that they both approach the problem from a single main line of insight. AOP is an intended approach for functional maintainability and AOM is a provision for the architectural dynamism of applications.

AOM proposes a pattern-based architecture (such as Composite, Interpreter, Builder) to define business entities, rules and relationships. However, its suggestions are only pattern-oriented and AOM does not define a generic framework for application development and deployment. Similarly the pattern-oriented approaches are somehow hard to achieve with the lack of proper programming models and associated software architectures.

We identified a set of business and architectural requirements that should be satisfied to develop flexible, reconfigurable and extendible software applications:

- Ease of development.
- Ease of change.
- Ease of administration.
- Ease of deployment: BR and CBL should be deployed separately. This deployment process should be "hot" enough so that there will be no shutdown and startup cycles in the middle tier.

So, a service-oriented meta-model is proposed as a solution for the requirements listed above, which can hold the definitions of CBL, BR and the relationships. In addition, implementations of CBL and BR will be based on AOM. Since AOM provides metadata information about CBL and BR classes, attributes will be based on instances rather than classes. This metadata information is used to form the meta-model. Both CBL and BR classes can use this metadata information to call each other.

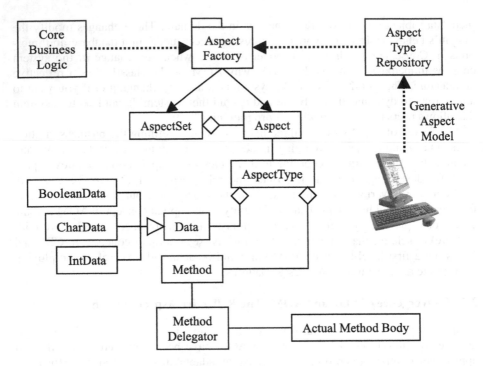

Fig. 3. Reflective Aspect Pattern for the Definition of Core Business Logic

Definition of CBL and BR entities should be designed in AOM such that the changes and new definitions can be integrated into the application without recompilation. In addition, the relationships should be changed dynamically. To this end, we propose the Reflective Aspect pattern depicted in Fig. 3.

Reflective Aspect pattern consists of:

– **Generative Aspect Model:** An aspect with reflective properties is nothing than a template definition of adaptive objects complying with AOM structure.
– **Aspect Factory** is a singleton in the core library so that it enables the creation of dynamic aspects at runtime in association with the templates kept in central Aspect Type Repository. Aspect Factory will be the gatekeeper for dynamic aspects in middleware to provide "zero deployment model" by instantiating the aspects from aspect templates kept in the Central Repository.
– **Aspect Type Repository** is composed of set of classes to keep the aspect templates to help Aspect Factory for the instantiation of reflective aspects accordingly. To this end, aspect definition screens will be the front-end of this Central Repository for defining and updating the templates.
– **Aspect (Template) Definition:** Aspect attributes, methods, hierarchy (aspect and sub-aspects) and the collaborations with other aspects are all definable through administrative screens.

- **Method Delegator:** Actual method implementers can be associated with dynamic aspects through the employment of Delegator pattern, which is very similar to Dynamic Behaviors pattern where different versions will be kept as a chain of responsibilities in the inherent behavior list. Associated generators can generate the final method calls for these delegators.

4 Rule-Based Model for Basic Aspects as Aurora Middleware

The Reflective Aspect pattern in the previous section provides the development and runtime management of the CBL with Zero Deployment Model. However, we also need a model in which business departments can simply define BR. To this end, we also propose a service-oriented meta-model called as Reflective Rule pattern (shown in Fig. 4) to manage BR and their relationships with reflective aspects.

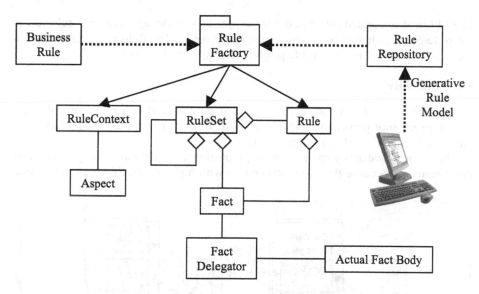

Fig. 4. Reflective Rule Pattern for the Definition of Business Rules

By following the principles given in the previous section, BR can be defined and managed similarly:

- **Generative Rule Model:** is very similar to Generative Aspect Model. Administrative screens will enable the users to define rules and rule-sets (set of rules that can be executed consecutively) through simple "if-then-else" structures. Actual fact implementations will be bound to rule and rule-set classes again with Delegator pattern.
- **Rule Factory:** is a singleton in the core library so that it enables the creation of dynamic rule and rule-sets in association with the templates kept in central repository.

- **Rule Repository:** is composed of a set of classes to keep the templates for Rule-sets and Rules to help Rule Factory for instantiating reflective Rules and Rule-sets accordingly. To this end, Rule **and** Rule-set definition screens will be the front-end of this Central Repository for defining and updating the templates.
- **Rule Context:** is the glue between aspect and rule/rule-set classes. If a service needs to execute a BR it will feed the facts as aspect attributes to the rule context and pass it to rule/rule-set classes. With this approach aspects and rules could be generated, deployed and managed separately.

Central Repository contains the definitions for aspects, properties, methods, method parameters, facts, rules, rule-set, rule-context, inter-relationship of repository items and generation settings.

5 Achieved Quality Factors

The SPL and integrated rule-based business process modeling have been selected as the system infrastructure for several enterprise projects. The following quality factors are mainly observed in the real-life projects discussed in Sect. 6.

5.1 Scalability

The scalability in the Aurora architecture can be achieved either by vertically (by adding processing power to a single hardware unit) or horizontally (by connecting other hardware units to form a logical unit).

The vertical scalability can produce a proportional throughput as long as you add more hardware because these systems end up with high-end machines and can make

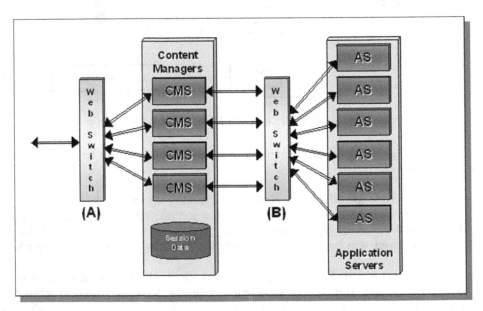

Fig. 5. Aurora Scalability Model

use of operating systems clustering facilities and hardware capabilities. But the amount of hardware that you can add to a single box is limited.

The horizontal scalability, on the other hand, is much more beneficial since it increases the system throughput by adding new hardware units while preserving the existing hardware investment. It is more difficult, however, to achieve near to linear scalability since addition of new hardware will increase the communication as well.

The Aurora scalability model is depicted in Fig 5. Content Management Servers (CMS) are clustered because they need to persist session state on a shared disk or in dedicated RDBMS. There is no interdependence among CMSs, they individually depend on the persistent space. The Web Switch (A) dispatches the incoming requests from the client based on "Source-IP Based Round Robin", which means as long as the CMS having the session state is alive Web Switch will dispatch the subsequent requests to that CMS, otherwise it will select another one using round robin approach.

When a request arrives to any CMS, it restores the session state data, attaches and delegates the request to Web Switch (B). Web Switch (B) delivers it to one of the Application Servers (AS) based on round robin again. The application servers need not to be clustered or on the same hardware box since there is no dependency among them. The request terminates in the AS instance and it starts executing the transaction.

The above model has been tested in several enterprise projects. The test results showed that the Aurora application model has near to linear scalability ($\%98.8$). This is due to the separation of CMS and AS instances and the elimination of dependency among CMS and AS instances.

5.2 7x24 Availability

As will be discussed in Sect. 6, the Aurora infrastructure has been used in several mission-critical enterprise applications including the core banking, insurance and central registry authority. Almost all of them require 7x24 availability since they all have access from different channels including the Internet.

The architectural model discussed in Sect. 5.1 also addresses the availability requirements of enterprise systems. The interdependency of content servers is limited to accessing the session state data that means if any content server fails the session state will be recovered from the common persistent session data. From the application server viewpoint, no dependency exists since they do not have any local state information and shared termination request for independent services.

6 Case Studies

This section briefly describes the enterprise projects having the Aurora architecture and RUMBA model. The common characteristics of these projects are having geographically distributed access channels, giving service to 1000+ users, executing complex and diverse business services, managing high volume of data and respective complexity, requiring power user capabilities over the Web, necessitating continuous and reliable interaction, running high volume of transactions especially at peak times, defining the 7x24 availability, having increased load over the time, and the need for B2B and B2C integration. Actually these characteristics expose the original design requirements of Aurora.

- **Core Banking System (CBS)** has been developed in approximately 2 years and completed in 3600 man-months. Java-based Core Banking Application is live for more than two years. The system has been integrated with more than 20 external system using XML/Web Service based adapters. The banking business model has been built on product and process concepts.
- **Central Registry Authority** has been developed in one and a half year with 400 man-months effort and has been in operation since the first quarter of 2005.
- **Insurance Project** is a very recent project where Aurora and the recently designed RUMBA model are being used. In this application, CBL is expressed in terms of basic aspects whereas the BR are defined using reflective rules and rule-sets by business departments. The prototype of the system (Customer Module) has been developed and succeeded in the preliminary tests.

The common architectural approaches employed by these projects are RIA with EBML presentation, SOA, Component-Based Development (CBD), Web Services for B2B integration and effective O2R mapping.

These systems have also changed the organization of IT departments so far. They have been reorganized according to the Aurora software development process, and dedicated teams are now responsible for requirement management, change management, configuration and release management, test management and issue tracking and quality management. Respective development teams, on the other hand, accomplish the design and development of application modules and they are less dependent on the members of other teams.

7 Conclusion

In this paper, we have introduced the Aurora SPL, which is a platform independent multi-tier Web architecture including core infrastructure based on RIA and EIA models for enterprise Web applications plus the software process management methodology, WYSIWYG design and development environments, configuration management techniques and tools. The projects having the Aurora architecture and achieved software quality factors have also been discussed.

Main contribution of the work is introduction of the "Reflective Aspect" and "Reflective Rule" patterns, which enable the integration of RUMBA with Aurora SPL. "Reflective Aspect" and "Reflective Rule" are architectural patterns proposing a "generative" model for basic aspects, rules and rule-sets designed thoroughly in AOM based on very simple delegated methods to be implemented by developers. The proposed model enables software development organizations to have a more capable SPL and/or better business process modeling together with the realization of separation of concerns for CBL and BR.

Our work continues with the construction of CBL/BR engine with high-level APIs and an associated powerful execution model. The engine will constitute an effective bridge between the presentation tier and rule-based application model. Another direction for the future research will be the formal assessment of Aurora SPL including the architectural, methodological, organization and project management concerns.

References

1. Phanouriou, Constantinos: UIML: A Device-Independent User Interface Markup Language. Ph.D. dissertation. http://scholar.lib.vt.edu/theses/available/etd-08122000-19510051/ (2000)
2. Hibernate. http://www.hibernate.org/
3. Duhl, J., The Business Impact of Rich Internet Applications. IDC White Paper. (2003)
4. Zubrow, Dave & Chastek, Gary: Measures for Software Product Lines, Technical Note CMU/SEI-2003-TN-031. (2003)
5. Clements, P. & Northrop, L. Software Product Lines: Patterns and Practice. Reading, MA: Addison Wesley. (2001)
6. Altintas, N. Ilker & Cetin, Semih. Aurora Software Product Line, in 2nd National Software Engineering Symposium. Ankara. (2005)
7. M. Aksit and B. Tekinerdogan, *Aspect-Oriented Programming Using Composition Filters*, in Object-Oriented Technology, S. Demeyer and J. Bosch (Eds.), ECOOP'98 Workshop Reader, Springer Verlag. (1998) pp 435
8. Anderson, Greg: Dynamic Behaviors in Java: Dynamically adapt program behaviors at runtime, December 27 2004, Last Retrieved 15 April 2005 http://www.javaworld.com/javaworld/jw-12-2004/jw-1227-behavior_p.html
9. L. Bergmans, M. Aksit and B. Tekinerdogan, *Aspect Composition Using Composition Filters*, in Software Architectures and Component Technology: The State of the Art in Research and Practice, M. Aksit (Ed.), Kluwer Academic Publishers, pp. 357 - 382, October 2001. (ISBN 0-7923-7576-9).
10. MetaData and Adaptive Object-Model, Last Retrieved 30 March 2005, http://www.adaptiveobjectmodel.com
11. D'Hont Maja, Hybrid Aspects for Integrating Rule-Based Knowledge and Object-Oriented Functionality. Ph.D. Thesis. System and Software Engineering Lab, Vrije Universiteit Brussel. (2004)
12. Dantas A. and Borba P. Adaptability Aspects: An Architectural Pattern for Structuring Adaptive Applications. In *Third Latin American Conference on Pattern Languages of Programming, SugarLoaf- PLoP'2003*, Brazil. (2003)
13. Northeastern University, College of Computer and Information Science, DemeterJ: Aspect-Oriented Software Development, 1996, Web address http://www.ccs.neu.edu/home/lieber/demeter.html
14. Elrad, T., Aksit, M., Kiczales, G., Lieberherr, K., Ossher, H.: Discussing Aspects of AOP. Communications of the ACM 44 (2001) 33–38
15. Filman, R.E., Elrad, T., Bader, A.: Aspect-Oriented Programming. Communications of the ACM 44 (2001) 29–32
16. IBM, HyperJ: Multi-Dimensional Separation of Concerns for Java, October 2001, Web address http://www.research.ibm.com/hyperspace/HyperJ/HyperJ.htm
17. Kiczales, G., Lamping, J., Mendhekar, A., Maeda, C., Lopes, C.V., Loingtier, J.M.,Irwin, J.: Aspect–Oriented Programming. In: European Conference on Object–Oriented Programming, ECOOP'97. LNCS 1241, Finland, Springer–Verlag (1997) 220–242
18. Ramnivas Laddad AspectJ in Action. Practical Aspect Oriented_Programming Manning Publications Co. ISBN 1-930110-93-6 2003
19. Yoder J. W., Balaguer F., & Johnson R.. "Architecture and Design of Adaptive Object Models" Intriguing Technology Presentation at the 2001 Conference on Object-Oriented Programming Systems, Languages, and Applications (OOPSLA '01), ACM SIGPLAN Notices, ACM Press, (2001).

20. Yoder J. W., Balaguer, F., & Johnson, R. "Adaptive Object Models for Implementing Business Rules" Position Paper for Third Workshop on Best-Practices for Business Rules Design and Implementation, OOPSLA (2001)
21. Erl, Thomas. Service-Oriented Architecture: A Field Guide to Integrating XML and Web Services. Prentice Hall. (2004)
22. Krafzig, D., Banke, K., & Slama, D. Enterprise SOA : Service-Oriented Architecture Best Practices (The Coad Series). Prentice Hall PTR. (2004)
23. Stevens, M., Service-Oriented Architecture, in Java Web Services Architecture, McGovern, J., Tyagi, S., Stevens, M., and Mathew, S., Morgan Kaufmann Publishers. (2003)
24. Stevens, W., Myers, G., and Constantine, L. Structured design. IBM System J. 13, 2. (1974) 115–139
25. Linthicum, D. S., Coupling Versus Cohesion: When to Leverage Services. (2004) Web Address http://www.ebizq.net/hot_topics/soa/features/4688.html
26. Linthicum, D. S., Enterprise Application Integration. Addison-Wesley Information Technology Series. (1999)
27. Cummins, F., Enterprise Integration: An Architecture for Enterprise Application and Systems Integration. Wiley. (2002)
28. O'Rourke, C., A Look at Rich Internet Applications. Oracle Magazine. (2004)
29. Grosso, W., Laszlo: An Open Source Framework for Rich Internet Applications. (2005) Web Address http://today.java.net/pub/a/today/2005/03/22/laszlo.html
30. Mullet, K., The Essence of Effective Rich Internet Applications. Macromedia Experience Design. (2003)

A Middleware Architecture for Supporting Adaptable Replication of Enterprise Application Data[*]

J.E. Armendáriz[1], H. Decker[2], F.D. Muñoz-Escoí[2],
L. Irún-Briz[2], and R. de Juan-Marín[2]

[1] Dpto. de Matemática e Informática, Universidad Pública de Navarra, Campus Arrosadía,
31006 Pamplona, Spain
[2] Instituto Tecnológico de Informática, Campus de Vera, 46022 Valencia, Spain
`enrique.armendariz@unavarra.es`,
`{hendrik, fmunyoz, lirun, rjuan}@iti.es`

Abstract. Enterprise-wide data replication improves availability, performance, fault-tolerance and dependability of database services within and between different subunits in medium and large enterprises. The overhead of consistency management of replicated data can be tamed by built-in DBMS functionality. Different kinds of applications, e.g., update-intensive online transaction processing, cyclical updates for data warehousing, knowledge sharing of repository data, and so on, have different requirements for the availability, up-to-dateness and consistency of replicated data. Thus, replication strategies should be adaptable to the specific requirements of diverse enterprise applications. We describe a middleware for enterprise-wide data replication. It maintains meta data for several protocols, so that the replication strategy can be adapted on the fly to the actual needs of an application.

1 Introduction

Medium- and large-sized enterprises are facing the challenge of making distributed information and related IT services highly available, performant and fault-tolerant, not only to external clients and customers but also to in-house users in business units as diverse as corporate and departmental administrations, planning, logistics, acquisition, production, sales, various levels of the management hierarchy, etc. Data replication has come to be a very promising way of boosting the availability, performance and fault tolerance of enterprise applications with underlying databases, including data warehouses, data marts or other kinds of data. Replication does not just consist of backup copies, which are usually off-line, but rather consists of a fully transparent on-line distribution of copies of entire databases or substantial parts thereof, including replication protocols and tradeoff policies to balance out requirements of availability and performance on one hand, and consistency of replica on the other.

Data-intensive enterprise applications typically range from frequently updated databases for online transaction processing applications, hourly or daily updated data warehouses, weekly or monthly updated data repositories, read-only services for external

---

[*] We acknowledge the support by the Spanish MCyT grant TIC2003-09420-C02 and the EU grant FP6-2003-IST-2-004152.

D. Draheim and G. Weber (Eds.): TEAA 2005, LNCS 3888, pp. 29–43, 2006.

mobile users, read- and write-access options for privileged internal users, and more. The availability, performance and fault tolerance of each of these databases, information systems and services is well-known to significantly benefit from replication.

However, two major hurdles need to be overcome when introducing replication for improving the availability, performance and fault tolerance of IT applications within and between diverse business units. The first is the error-prone complexity of developing suitable replication protocols, as well as the overhead produced by such protocols for maintaining the consistency of replicated data [3]. For business-critical applications, this can easily amount to a severe impediment.

The second obstacle which may prevent the use of replication in enterprise applications is that different departments use different services and have different requirements on the consistency and availability of corporate data. For instance, for the strategic planning of an airline enterprise, the statistics delivered by a data warehouse typically do not rely on most recent updates to business data. Rather, statistics are generated in overnight or background processes. They refer to stable database states reached at well-defined breakpoints (e.g., at the end of the previous day), without taking into account currently ongoing transactions. On the other hand, booking and sales services for online flight reservations need to be based on up-to-date database states. In general, different classes of applications and users possibly have different requirements on the accuracy, replication consistency, timeliness and availability of the underlying data. However, distributed databases typically support at most just a single manner of replication, a fixed consistency maintenance scheme and a uniform policy for availability and failover management. A more flexible replication architecture which can be adapted to the changing needs of different applications and users is therefore desirable.

In this paper, we describe the middleware MADIS, with an emphasis on its suitability for enterprise applications [6]. It enhances the availability, performance, fault-tolerance and dependability of business applications by enterprise-wide database replication. "Enterprise-wide" implies that replication in both local- and wide-area networks is supported. Both can be combined seamlessly, which is important for a smooth interoperation of intra- and extranet applications.

Our middleware overcomes the two stumbling blocks mentioned above. With regard to the first, standard SQL constructs (views, triggers etc) and ready-made SQL functionality (schema definition, trigger firing etc) are used for implementing major parts of the meta data handling and the network communication of the protocols. That way, the protocols themselves become much less cluttered and thus much easier to develop and implement. With regard to the second, MADIS simultaneously maintains meta data for several protocols, so that the replication strategy can be adapted seamlessly. Suitable protocols can be chosen, plugged in and exchanged on the fly in order to adapt to the actual needs of given applications.

Section 2 describes the overall architecture, emphasising the adaptability of replication strategies and the pluggability of protocols. Section 3 showcases different configurations of the middleware. Section 4 describes the use of standard SQL functionality for decreasing the overhead of meta data management and replication consistency. Section 5 outlines an implementation of the replication consistency management as a standard JDBC driver. Section 6 experimentally verifies the performance advantage claimed in

Sect. 4. Section 7 provides a review of recent works addressing replication of enterprise data. Finally, Sect. 8 concludes the paper.

2 Architecture

The architecture is two-layered, see Fig. 1. It makes consistency management independent of any DBMS particularities. MADIS takes advantage of ready-made database resources so that protocol overhead is kept to a minimum. The replication strategy is adaptable, and thus more dependable, since the architecture allows for plugging in suitable protocols that fit given applications best.

The upper layer consists of replication management functions, while the lower one of a mechanism for extending the original database schema. The extension exclusively uses standard SQL constructs such as view definitions and triggers. The upper layer handles transaction requests from users or applications and uses the report tables for transparent replication management. Meta data of database records involved in transactions are automatically stored in particular tables of the extended schema, called *report tables*. Thus, meta data handling becomes much simpler. The upper layer processes transaction requests from users or applications by making use of the report tables for transparent replication management. The upper layer can be implemented in any programming language with a SQL interface, since its functionality exclusively relies on standard SQL constructs executed by the underlying DBMS.

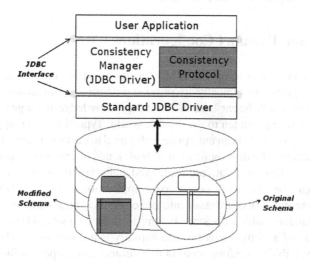

Fig. 1. Layered MADIS architecture

The report tables account for transactions in the local node, and are updated within the transactions accounted for. The schema extension also includes some stored procedures which hide some schema extension details to the upper layer. The latter is sandwiched between client applications and database, acting as a database mediator. Accesses to the database as well as commit/rollback requests are intercepted, such that the replication protocol can transparently do its work. The protocol may access the report tables to obtain information about transactions, in order to cater for required consistency guarantees. The protocol may also manipulate the extended schema using stored procedures.

Of course, the performance of such a middleware will always tend to be somewhat worse than that of a core-based solution, such as Postgres-R [11], but its advantage is to be independent of the given database and easily portable to other DBMSs.

The implementation of the consistency manager CM, i.e., the core of MADIS, is independent of the underlying database. In Sect. 5, we describe a Java implementation, to be used by client applications as a common JDBC driver. Its consistency control functionality is provided transparently to users and applications. The CM handles transaction requests, including multiple sequential transactions in different JDBC consistency modes, and communicates with database replicas. It provides the plug-in for the replication protocol chosen according to given needs and requirements. All supported protocols share some common characteristics. Communication between the database replicas is controlled by the CM which is local to each network node.

MADIS supports the pluggability of protocols, i.e., a suitable protocol (e.g., with eager or lazy update propagation, optimistic or pessimistic concurrency control, etc) can be freely chosen, plugged in and exchanged, according to the shifting needs of given applications, even at runtime. Protocol switching is seamless and fast, since the meta data for each protocol in the MADIS repertoire is readily at hand at plug-in time. In Sect. 3, we outline different configuration scenarios of the middleware in which different replication protocols are plugged in.

3   Intranet and Extranet Configurations

Enterprise applications can be classified as services for either internal or external purposes. Internal applications typically are intranet enterprise applications, e.g., IT-based collaboration between different business units, or knowledge management, which is open for internal use but hidden to the outside world. Typical external applications are extranet services, provided via an enterprise web portal to customers and clients. MADIS can be used to support the data replication of both kinds of enterprise applications.

For intranet applications, data are replicated transparently at each user site. Such configurations can be likened to peer-to-peer applications. On the other hand, using MADIS for data replication of extranet enterprise services means that external users access a virtual database which does not belong to their own site. Thus, extranet users behave as clients of a virtual server which actually is a transparently distributed system the high availability, performance, fault tolerance and dependability of which is supported by a transparent replication architecture.

As shown in Fig. 2, intranet and extranet application scenarios can be interoperated orthogonally. Users of one or several extranet MADIS-supported enterprise applications may at the same time use replicas of one or several intranet applications relying on transparently replicated data. Then, installations of MADIS for intranet and extranet application support can (and should) be independently tuned according to their own particular requirements. In particular, different protocols can be plugged into different

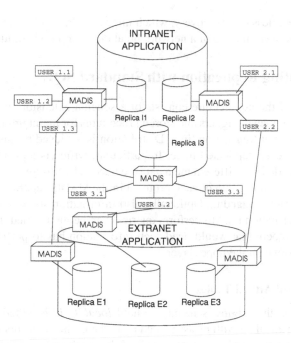

Fig. 2. Intranet and extranet application support

installations of the middleware for different applications, for simultaneously meeting different requirements of availability and replication consistency.

Web-based collaboration may serve as an example of a combination of intranet and extranet applications. For instance, external collaboration partners (e.g., customers or business partners) may use an application driven by an enterprise-owned web server for scheduling a web meeting and locating other partners. Suppose that, for making this application highly available, performant, fault-tolerant and dependable, the underlying data are replicated by MADIS. Further, suppose that the processes and data for running the actual web meeting are served by an internal application, the data of which are also replicated among the different participants of the enterprise, as pictured in Fig. 2 (the large cylinders suggests that users perceive distributed replicas, represented by small cylinders, as a single system). Then, the extranet application is probably best served by a replication protocol that guarantees a very high degree of data consistency, since the scheduling data are supposed to be accurate at any time. On the other hand, replication protocols for the database in the intranet can possibly be more relaxed. This is because it neither really matters nor is possible at all that the latest version of shared collaboration data are always immediately replicated and displayed on each screen at the very same time. Rather, delays of up to some seconds are usually tolerable in data communication for web-based collaboration. Hence, protocols used in the intranet may take advantage of such delays by allowing to slightly defer activities for achieving consistency of all replica.

Relaxation of consistency can then be conveniently traded off in favour of other virtues of the protocols. For instance, a higher precaution can be taken in terms of failure prevention and seamless error recovery, which improves the availability of shared data as well as their recovery in case of a network breakdown or a node failure.

4   Implementing Replication with Standard SQL

The lower layer of the architecture consists of a schema extension of the underlying database, including views, triggers and stored procedures for maintaining records about activities performed at transaction time. Distribution is achieved by migrating the extended schema to each replicated node. In particular, writesets and other transaction meta data are recorded. As different meta data are needed by different protocols, the extension caters for the meta data of each protocol in the MADIS repertoire, also of those that are currently not plugged in. Optionally, also information about readsets (possibly including the information read to perform queries) can be maintained. If that option is not taken, any protocol that would need such information has to perform some work that otherwise is done on the upper layer.

4.1   Modified and Added Tables

To each table T_i in the original schema, the field $local\_T_i\_id$ is added for identifying and linking each row of T_i with its associated meta data. This identifier is local to each node, i.e., each row may have different $local\_T_i\_id$'s distributed over the network. Each row also has a unique global identifier, composed of the row's creator node ID and the row identifier local to that node, which is equal in all replicas.

For each T_i, a table $Meta\_T_i$ is created, containing the meta data for any replication protocol in the repertoire. $Meta\_T_i$ contains

- **local_id:** local identifier; primary key.
- **global_id:** unique global identifier.
- **version:** the row's version number.
- **transaction_id:** ID of the last transaction that updated the row.
- **timestamp:** most recent date the row was locally updated.

In general, it contains all the information needed by any protocol in the MADIS repertoire. Hence, as all fields are maintained by the database manager, any such protocol is suitable to be plugged in deliberately.

In addition to meta tables, the table *TrReport* is defined, containing a log of all transactions, with the following attributes:

- **tr_id:** transaction identifier; part of primary key.
- **global_id:** global row identifier; part of primary key.
- **field_id:** optional accessed field identifier; part of primary key.
- **mode:** access mode (read/insert/delete/modify).

For each transaction τ, one record for each field of each row involved in τ is maintained in *TrReport*. Once a transaction τ is committed, the consistency manager eliminates any information related to τ from *TrReport*. Note that several MVCC-based DBMSs do not use locks with row granularity, but block access to entire pages or even tables. Such systems must use multiple "per transaction" temporary *TrReport* tables.

4.2 Triggers

The set of trigger definitions introduced by MADIS in the schema can be classified into three groups:

- *Writeset managers* for collecting information related to rows written by transactions.
- *Readset managers* for collecting information related to rows read by transactions; their inclusion is optional and depends on the replication protocol being used.
- *Metadata automation* for updating meta data in meta tables.

The writeset collection uses, for each table T_i in the original schema, triggers which insert information related to write-accesses to T_i at transaction time in *TrReport*.

The following example shows such a trigger, for the insertion into *mytab* (say). With *getTr_id()*, it gets the transaction's identifier. A row is inserted in the *TrReport* table for each insertion to *mytable*, in order to keep track of the transaction. Deletions and updates are handled analogously.

```
CREATE TRIGGER WSC_insert_mytab
BEFORE INSERT ON mytab
FOR EACH ROW EXECUTE PROCEDURE
tr_insert(mytab,getTrid(),NEW.l_mytab_id)
```

Collecting readsets is optional, due to high costs and also because some protocols can do without readsets. Costs are high since the implementation must laboriously compensate for a lack of a *TRIGGER...BEFORE SELECT* construct in the SQL-99 standard.

Another group of triggers is responsible for the meta data management. Whenever a row is inserted, such a trigger also inserts the row in the meta data table $Meta\_T_i$. Since the row's *global_id* (i.e. the global identifier of the new data item), can be generated from the row's node creator identifier and a local sequence value in the creator node (maintained in another MADIS meta table), all fields in $Meta\_T_i$ can be filled without intervention of any consistency protocol.

Whenever a row is accessed in write mode, another MADIS trigger updates the meta data of that row in the corresponding meta table, i.e., it updates the *version*, the *transaction identifier*, and *timestamp* of the record in the given meta data table. Conversely, whenever a row is deleted, the corresponding meta data row is also deleted, by yet another MADIS trigger.

In summary, MADIS adds, for each table, three triggers, of type BEFORE INSERT, BEFORE UPDATE, BEFORE DELETE, which cater for transaction report management and meta data maintenance. Optionally, for readset management, the *INSTEAD OF* trigger construct must be used, for redirecting write accesses to appropriate tables.

5 Implementing Replication as a JDBC Driver

MADIS makes use of ready-made SQL functionality for consistency management. Automatically generated database triggers collect information about accesses at transaction time for the CM, which in turn is independent of the DBMS. Thus, the CM can be ported from one platform to another with minimal effort. This Section sketches a Java implementation of CM and how it makes use of the MADIS schema modification.

In our prototype, a JDBC driver encapsulates an existing PostgreSQL driver, for intercepting user application requests. They are augmented to new request for taking care of the meta data associated to the arguments of the requests. Meta data handling is completely hidden from users and applications. The plugged-in protocol is notified about any application request to the database, including query execution, row recovery, transaction termination (i.e. commit/rollback), etc. Thus, the protocol can easily accomplish its tasks regarding replication consistency.

MADIS intercepts queries by encapsulating the *Statement* class. Responding to *createStatement* or *prepareStatement* calls, MADIS generates statements that take care of query execution. For each user application query request, MADIS calls the *processStatement()* operation of the currently plugged-in protocol. The latter updates the transaction report, and may modify the statement by adding the patches needed to retrieve some meta data. However, such modifications are only needed by a few consistency protocols, since the meta data can be retrieved from the report tables, once the original query has been completed. Optimistic consistency protocols do not need such meta data before the transaction has requested a commit. The query execution process is shown in Fig. 3. Figure 4 describes the update control flow.

Whenever, for a transaction, the user or application requests a *commit* or when a *rollback* is invoked, MADIS notifies the protocol, which thus has the opportunity to involve any replica nodes for satisfying the request. If the protocol concludes its activity

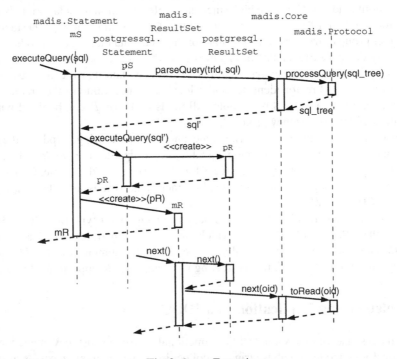

Fig. 3. Query Execution

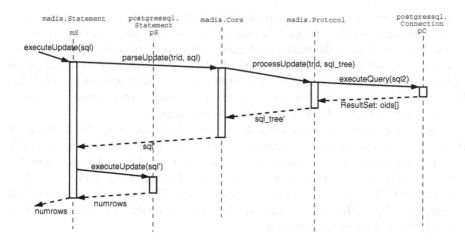

Fig. 4. Update Execution

with a positive result, then the transaction is ready to commit in the local database, and the CM is notified accordingly, who in turn responds to the user application. Any negative result obtained from the protocol will be notified directly to the application, after the abortion of the local transaction. Similarly, *rollback()* requests are also intercepted, redirected to the CM and forwarded to the protocol.

6   Performance Evaluation

A key idea of our architecture is that, instead of the protocols, the DBMS is responsible for generating and maintaining the information needed by the protocols for accomplishing consistency maintenance, concurrency control and update propagation. Now, questions arise about the costs of storage space and computation time of this solution, which involves several schema modifications and additional queries, resulting in some overhead. In Sect. 6.1 we display performance evaluation results for MADIS and in Sect.6.2 we compare MADIS with other related approaches.

6.1   Measuring MADIS

The overhead of storage space needed for the schema modification (i.e., definitions of views, triggers and stored procedures) is marginal. The main portion of space consumption is due to the $Meta\_T_j$ tables. Apart from containing two identifiers (local and global object id), these tables allocate space for the meta data of each of the pluggable protocols in the MADIS repertoire. These include transaction identifiers, timestamps, sequential version numbers and transaction reports. The space needed for that is easily afforded, since it scales linearly with the product of the number of protocols and transactions.

Some computational overhead is generated by additional SQL statements and calculations executed by MADIS for each database access. Insertions (I), Updates (U) and deletions (**D**) involve additional insertions in the *TrReport* table, plus some operations on corresponding *Meta_T_j* tables. The overhead for select statements depends on the protocol. In most cases, the readset collection can be performed by the middleware. amounting to nothing more than including the *local_id* in the SELECT clause of the SQL statements to be executed. Below, we discuss the overhead introduced in *I*, *U* and *D* operations in more detail. For a fair evaluation, we used a very simple protocol, in order to focus on the overhead introduced by the architecture.

Test runs consisted in executing a Java programme, accessing the database via JDBC. The programme has two parameters: *numtr*, the number of transactions to be executed, and *numrows*, the number of rows to be manipulated by each transaction. The schema used in the test runs contains the four tables *CUSTOMER, SUPPLIER, ARTI-CLE* and *ORDER*. Each article references a row in the *SUPPLIER* table. Each *ORDER* references a *CUSTOMER* row and an *ARTICLE* row. Each table contains an additional *varchar[30]* field for item description.

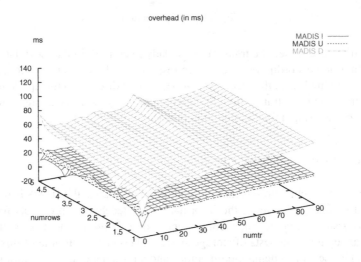

Fig. 5. MADIS absolute overhead (in ms)

After establishing the database connection and the extended schema, each test run executes some "training" transactions, including the loading of all Java classes needed. Then, the time taken by *numtr* sequential transactions (performing a number of insertions, updates or deletions depending on the required measurement) is measured. This yields the total cost of the *numtr* transactions of type *I*, *U* and *D*, respectively. For accurately capturing the overhead, we measured the absolute and relative time needed per transaction as it is shown in Figs. 5 and 6.

The results stabilised with a few number of transactions, which indicates that the system does not suffer appreciable performance degradation over time. In addition, Fig. 5 shows that the overhead per transaction is always lower than 80ms in our experiments. Figure 6 shows that the size of the *numrows* parameter is negligible (i.e., the system scales well when the number of table rows grows) for any of the transaction types *I*, *U* and *D*. It turned out that the MADIS database core introduces a limited

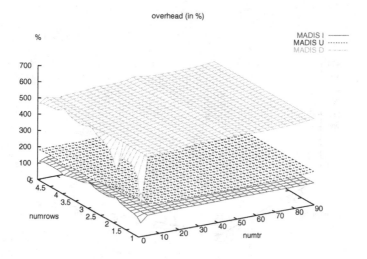

Fig. 6. MADIS relative overhead (in %)

overhead for insertions and update operations. Deletions, however, may produce a log-arithmic, though non-negligible performance degradation. For instance, deleting 6000 rows took about 6 times more time as the same deletions in the unmodified schema.

6.2 Other Approaches

The middleware COPLA [10] of the GlobData project [14] was used as an R&D platform on which several replication protocols were developed and implemented. COPLA also permits the pluggability of protocols, but, as opposed to MADIS, only at well-defined breakpoints between different sessions, i.e., not on the fly. In particular, there was no

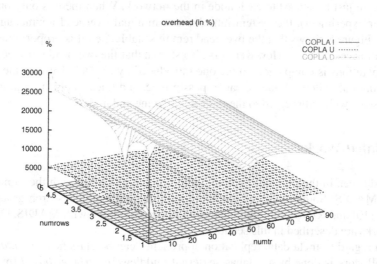

Fig. 7. Relative COPLA/MADIS overhead

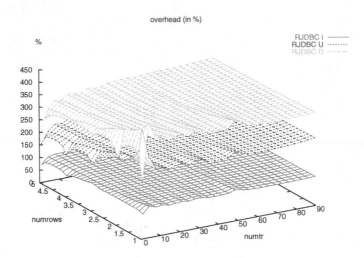

Fig. 8. Relative MADIS/RJDBC overhead

simultaneous management of meta data for several protocols. Moreover, the meta data management for the plugged-in protocol was not handled via a schema extension,but was integrated within the protocol's code. This, together with a burdensome mapping from an object-oriented user interface to the underlying relational database structures resulted in a costly performance. For comparing MADIS with COPLA, we ran the same transactions in equivalent configurations. As shown in Fig. 7, the scalability of COPLA for update and delete operations was 50 and, respectively, 200 times more costly than in MADIS.

We also compared MADIS to RJDBC [2], which effectively constitutes a lower bound of achievable results. In RJDBC, no metadata are maintained. Instead, all requests to the database are just broadcast to each node in the network. When there is only one node (as in our experiment), the system introduces a minimal overhead for managing the requests. Figure 8 shows that the overhead remains stable, i.e., it is proportional to the number of accessed rows. However, it is also shown that the overhead introduced for I and U operations is comparable to the one introduced by MADIS. Thus, as the RJDBC architecture only allows a unique eager, pessimistic, and linear replication protocol, it will not scale well with regard to the number of connected nodes.

7   Related Works

As already seen in the previous Section, there are many systems with the same objectives as MADIS. Some of them have been implemented by our research groups, like COPLA [10] and RJDBC [2], that have been compared above with MADIS. Other related works are described in this section.

With regard to meta data, replication approaches can be classified as *middleware-based* (all work is done by a database-external middleware), *trigger-based* (meta data are collected by triggers and calls to external procedures), *shadow-table-based* (using shadow copies to build update messages for replicas), and *control-table-based* (timestamping each row). Benefits and drawbacks of each are discussed in [15, 16]. Therefore, MADIS is enclosed inside the *middleware-based* approach.

In Postgres-R and Dragon [12, 17], a DBMS core is modified to support distribution. This approach strongly depends on the underlying DBMS thus being not portable, and must be reviewed for each new DBMS release. However, its performance is generally better than a middleware architecture. Recently, these systems have been ported to a middleware architecture [13], introducing a minimal support in the DBMS core in order to access its internal redo-logs for obtaining (or applying) the writesets of the currently executing transactions (or those of the remote transactions that have been locally delivered, respectively). This core support also simplifies a lot the work to be done in the middleware, reducing the overall costs needed for such a management, at least when compared to our MADIS approach that uses triggers to this end. As a result, this Postgres-R evolution has better performance than MADIS, but MADIS only uses standard SQL features and is easier to port to other DBMSs.

Solutions based on Java, implemented as JDBC drivers, can be found in C-JDBC [1, 4] and RJDBC [2]. The latter has been already described above. The former emphasises load balancing but is also able to provide support for fault-tolerance. To this end, this system is able to make checkpoints of the current state of the replicated database and it also uses a recovery log for bringing failed replicas up-to-date when they recover. Moreover, in the regular executions of the system, all update operations are delivered to all existing replicas, whilst read operations only access one of the replicas, using a load balancer for improving the overall system performance. C-JDBC also shares with MADIS its easy portability to different platforms and DBMSs, since it only needs a JDBC native driver for accessing the underlaying databases, and it uses standard JDBC features.

Progress DataXtend RE (formerly known as PeerDirect) [15] uses triggers and procedures for replication, but no other than a predefined protocol is usable in that system. Additionally, the new editions of this software have migrated their focus to mobile environments, being able to provide different levels of consistency among the set of replicas of a given piece of data.

Finally, ORION Integrator [7] is another commercial tool that also provides support for data replication and integration. However, its aim is not exactly the same as that of the previously discussed research projects [1, 10, 17] or commercial products. It is similar to them, since it also provides support for replication, but it needs that each replicated item has a *source* replica and one or many *target* replicas, configured as such. On the other hand, this product is able to achieve an easy integration of different DBMSs, i.e., different replicas may use different underlying DBMSs. Its core engine is able to translate the data when it is being propagated in order to store it in the appropriate format for its target DBMS.

8   Conclusion

Data replication is an effective means to enhance performance, fault-tolerance, availability, and thus dependability, of enterprise applications. Different applications require different kinds of replication management. Hence, an adequate choice of appropriate protocols is due. Hence, a middleware which provides flexible support for choosing, plugging in, operating and exchanging suitable protocols is desirable for many applications. This innovative kind of pluggability is being realized in MADIS. It has an ample repertoire of replication protocols, each with particular consistency guarantees, from which suitable ones can be chosen, plugged in and exchanged on the fly. The implementation makes use of standard SQL-99 constructs such as table alterations, views, constraints, triggers and stored procedures. That way, protocols can be developed and implemented much more efficiently than in comparable middleware packages, where the meta data management for maintaining the consistency of replicated data either is opaquely intertwined in the protocol's code or, worse, is hidden in the application code. Moreover, the protocol's structure becomes much more elegant and concise when the meta data management is largely delegated to the underlying DBMS, as in MADIS. These conceptual advantages have been verified by experimental measurements.

Experimental results of the prototype implementation appear in [9], and more implementation details in [8]. The project DeDiSys [5] currently serves as a benchmarking scenario for MADIS.

The ease of developing new protocols is expected to bear fruit also for an envisaged extension of the middleware with functionality for supporting mobile users. This requires the development of new protocols with enhanced capabilities of coping with more unstable networks, narrower bandwidths, greater heterogenity of platforms and devices, etc.

References

1. E. Cecchet, J. Marguerite, W. Zwaenepoel. C-JDBC: Flexible database clustering middleware. Proc. of the FREENIX Track: 2004 USENIX Annual Technical Conference, Boston, MA, USA. 9-18, July 2004.
2. J. Esparza, F. Muñoz, L. Irún, J. Bernabéu: RJDBC, a simple database replication engine. *Proc. 6th ICEIS*, 587-590, 2004.
3. J. Gray, P. Helland, P. O'Neil, and D. Shasha: The dangers of replication and a solution. *Proc. ACM SIGMOD*, 173-182, 1996.
4. *http://c-jdbc.objectweb.org*, downloaded 19 October 2005.
5. *http://www.dedisys.org*, downloaded 19 October 2005.
6. *http://www.iti.upv.es/madis/*, downloaded 19 October 2005.
7. *http://www.orionintegrator.com*, downloaded 19 October 2005.
8. L. Irún, J. Armendáriz, H. Decker, J. González de Mendívil, F. Muñoz: Replication Tools in the MADIS Middleware. *Proc. VLDB'05 Workshop on Design, Implementation and Deployment of Database Replication*, 25-32, 2005.
9. L. Irún, H. Decker, R. de Juan, F. Castro, J. Armendáriz, F. Muñoz: MADIS: A Slim Middleware for Database Replication. *Proc. 11th Euro-Par*, LNCS 3648, 349-359, 2005.
10. L. Irún, F. Muñoz, H. Decker, J. Bernabéu: COPLA: A Platform for Eager and Lazy Replication in Networked Databases. *Proc. 5th ICEIS*, Vol. 1, 273-278, 2003.
11. B. Kemme: *Database Replication for Clusters of Workstations*. PhD thesis, ETH Zurich, 2000.
12. B. Kemme, G. Alonso: A Suite of Database Replication Protocols based on Group Communication Primitives. *Proc. Distributed Computing Systems*, 156-163, 1988.

13. Y. Lin, B. Kemme, M. Patiño-Martínez, R. Jiménez-Peris. Middleware Based Data Replication Providing Snapshot Isolation *Proc. ACM SIGMOD*, 419-430, 2005.
14. F.D. Muñoz-Escoí, L. Irún-Briz, P. Galdámez, J.M. Bernabéu-Aubán, J. Bataller, and M.C. Bañuls: GlobData: Consistency Protocols for Replicated Databases. *Proc. YUFORIC'2001*, 97-104, 2001.
15. Overview & Comparison of Data Replication Architectures. *Peer Direct* whitepaper, Nov. 2002.
16. Replication Strategies: Data Migration, Distribution and Synchronization. *Sybase* whitepaper, Nov. 2003.
17. S. Wu, B. Kemme: Postgres-R(SI): Combining Replica Control with Concurrency Control based on Snapshot Isolation. *Proc. IEEE ICDE*, Tokio, Japan, Apr. 2005.

MDA and Analysis of Web Applications

Behzad Bordbar and Kyriakos Anastasakis

School of Computer Science, University of Birmingham,
Birmingham, B15 2TT, UK
{B.Bordbar, K.Anastasakis}@cs.bham.ac.uk

Abstract. Enterprise systems are mission critical. As a result, ensuring their correctness is of primary concern. This paper aids to the analysis of Web applications, focusing on the aspects related to the interaction of business logic and Web browsers. The method adopted is based on the Model Driven Architecture. First, the Platform Independent Model of Web applications is refined to create a new model called Abstract Description of Interaction (ADI). An ADI is a UML class diagram annotated with OCL statements to represent an abstraction of the interaction between the thin client and the business logic. Secondly, the ADI model is automatically transferred to an Alloy model and analysed using the Alloy Analyser.

1   Introduction

Over the past two decades Web applications have become increasingly vital, affecting almost all aspects of our daily life such as banking, retail, information gathering, entertainment and learning. Such applications are mostly mission critical [1]. Hence, ensuring the correctness of the specification and implementation is a primary concern and has received considerable attention [2, 3, 4]. To analyse these systems, it is important to create a formal model. For example, [2] uses μ-calculus to represent the model, while [3] makes use of a variant of automata as the analyzable model. Stotts and Navon [4] present a model based on Petri nets. Our approach makes use of MDA [5, 6, 7] transformations to automatically create the analysable model. Existing approaches [2, 3, 4] either consider static Web sites or analyse applications that have already been implemented. In contrast we use a formalism [8], which is ideal [9] for the analysis of the models of object oriented systems, such as Web applications.

This paper aids to the analysis of Web applications [10]; software applications, which are accessed via Web browsers. In particular, we are interested in identifying bugs such as the Amazon bug [11] and the Orbitz bug [12], which are created as a result of the interaction between browsers and the business logic. Figure 1 sketches our approach.

The MDA [5, 6, 7] emphasises on the role of models by capturing high level abstraction of the system that is independent of any implementation platform, called Platform Independent Model (PIM). A PIM is then transformed to one or more Platform Specific Model (PSM) via an MDA tool. A PSM specifies the

D. Draheim and G. Weber (Eds.): TEAA 2005, LNCS 3888, pp. 44–55, 2006.

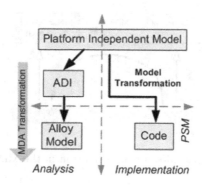

Fig. 1. Implementation and Analysis via MDA

system in a particular implementation technology, platform and paradigm. There are already commercial [13] and non-commercial [14] MDA tools facilitating the implementation of a large part of the code on various choices of platform and programming languages. To analyse the model, the PIM has to be refined and abstracted to create a new PIM which we shall refer to as Abstract Description of Interaction (ADI). The ADI is a class diagram [15] with a set of OCL [16] constraints and pre and post condition expressions, that describes the interaction of the browser and the business logic in an abstract way. The ADI model can be translated to a model in Alloy [8] and analysed by the Alloy Analyser [17]. We have implemented the transformation from the UML to Alloy in a tool called UML2Alloy [18, 19].

The paper is organised as follows. Section 2 presents a brief introduction to MDA, Alloy and UML2Alloy. Section 3 sketches a method for the creation of the ADI. To demonstrate our approach, Sect. 4 analyses an example of an e-commerce system. Finally in Sect. 5 we sketch the related work and future direction, while Sect. 6 provides the conclusions of our work.

2   Preliminaries

Model Driven Architecture (MDA) [5, 6, 7] is a framework proposed by the Object Management Group [20]. Central to the MDA is the idea of model transformation, which maps models in a *source* language into a model expressed in a *destination* language. Models in the MDA are instances of *metamodels*. A metamodel is in effect a model that describes another model. The Meta Object Facility (MOF) [21] specifies the layered architecture that the MDA follows, where each model is an instance of its metamodel. As depicted by Fig. 2, an MDA transformation is defined from the source metamodel to the destination metamodel. Then every model, which is an instance of the corresponding metamodel, can be transformed to an instance of the destination metamodel. For example, to map a UML class diagram to Alloy, an MDA transformation that maps the metamodel of Class diagrams to the metamodel of the Alloy language is required. An MDA tool is a tool that implements a model transformation. In other words, it receives

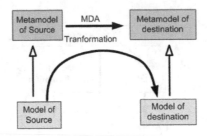

Fig. 2. Model transformation in the MDA

a description of the metamodels of the source and destination and a specification of the model transformation rules and for every model that conforms to the source metamodel, it generates a corresponding model, which is an instance of the target metamodel.

2.1   Alloy

Alloy [8] is a textual modelling language based on first order predicate logic [22]. An Alloy model is made of a number of *Signatures*, which describe the entities in the model. Signatures are similar to classes in a UML class diagram. For example a Signature can define *Fields* which are like Attributes of classes in UML class diagrams.

There are also three major kinds of expressions in an Alloy model. A *Fact* is an expression that every instance of a model satisfies. *Predicates* and *Functions* are like functions in an object oriented programming language. They can be invoked from other parts of the model. Finally an *assertion* is a statement that the modeller wants to check for its validity. Alloy models are analysable and Alloy Analyzer [17], which is an implementation supporting the Alloy language, can present a *counterexample* if an assertion is violated.

Alloy tackles the state explosion problem [23] by introducing scoped analysis. A *scope* is the maximum number of stages the Alloy Analyzer probes to ensure the validity of an assertion or to find the existence of counterexamples. If the Alloy Analyzer fails to come up with a counterexample, the assertion may be valid. The bigger the scope is, the more confident the modeller is that his model is correct. For further details on the Alloy language the interested reader is referred to [8].

2.2   Analysis of UML Models Via UML2Alloy

The UML is a family of languages that is prevailing in the modelling and specification of object oriented systems. The UML defines a number of diagrams [15], some of which depict the static structure of a system, while others the dynamic aspect. In this paper, we shall make use of UML class diagrams to model the static structure of a system. We shall describe the behaviour of the system via OCL [16]. OCL is a textual language that adds formalism to UML diagrams. It can be used to define the behaviour of a model (with the use of *preconditions* and *postconditions*) or to express constraints (using *invariants*) on the elements of a UML model.

Based on the MDA, we have developed a CASE tool called *UML2Alloy* for automating the translation of UML models to the corresponding Alloy models. Figure 3 depicts the sequence of steps involved in the transformation. The starting point is to create a UML model of the system in a UML CASE tool such as ArgoUML [24]. Most UML tools, including ArgoUML, can export the UML model to an XMI [25] format. XMI, which stands for XML Metadata Interchange is an OMG standard used by most UML tools to store, import and export UML models. UML2Alloy implements the transformation and generates an Alloy model from the XMI file. The Alloy model of the system can then be analysed with the Alloy Analyser [17]. For further details on UML2Alloy, we refer the reader to [18, 19].

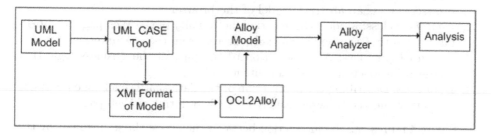

Fig. 3. Process of Analysis of UML models via UML2Alloy

In the following Section we shall present a method of verifying enterprise Web applications with the help of UML2Alloy.

3 Analysis of the Interaction Between a Browser and Business Logic

A Web application is a software application that is accessible via a thin client (Web browser). Web applications often consist of multiple tiers; the presentation tier (Web server), application tier (business logic) and resource management (data) tier. Web applications render Web pages, comprising of different kinds information (e.g. text, images, forms) and are accessed via Web browsers. Web pages can be *static* (i.e. residing on a Web server) or *dynamic* (i.e. modifiable as a result of the execution of various scripts and components at the client or the server). As a result models of Web applications are very large and complex, involving numerous components. Consequently, to conduct any realistic analysis, it is crucial to get rid of the unrelated information and create an abstract model capturing the interaction between the browser and the business logic. To do so, we shall introduce a new class model called Abstract Description of Interaction (ADI). The following sketches the steps involved in the creation of the ADI.

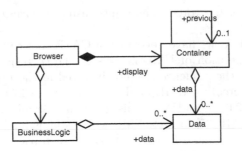

Fig. 4. A template for Abstract Description Interaction

1. *Browser* class: A model of the browser with its related functionality, such as navigating between various pages using the *back* and *forward* buttons. The browser class is an abstract model of the browser.
2. *Container* class: Models the generic functionality of the Web pages comprising of data that can be dynamically altered from the user interface.
3. *BusinessLogic* class: An abstraction of the part of the business logic that relates to browser and its data content.
4. *Data* class: Describing the abstraction of the data that is exchanged between the server and the browser usually as fields of forms of Web pages.

Figure 4 represents the interaction between the above classes inspired by the general form of Web applications, in which:

- A *Browser* displays a *Container*.
- A *Container* can have a *previous Container*. To simplify we have not included a *next Container*.
- A *Browser* interacts with the *BusinessLogic*.
- A *Container* displays *Data* units
- A BusinessLogic deals with a number of *Data* units.

The template of Fig. 4 and the steps sketched above can allow the modeller to probe the PIM and create the ADI. Platform Independent Models of Web applications are large and complex. Hence, finding methods of a partial automation of the creation of the ADI is of paramount importance. Since the creation of the ADI involves the projection of the model and the deletion of unrelated model elements, we speculate that it might be possible to mark unrelated model elements on the PIM and refactor [26] the model to create the ADI, or a model near enough to the ADI. However that remains an area for future research. For now, to demonstrate examples of the creation of the ADI, we shall present a case study.

4   Analysis of an e-Commerce System: A Case Study

This case study is inspired by [27]. The class diagram of Fig. 5 represents a portion of the PIM of an internet bookstore system, extracted from [27, p. 120–123], which describes how the model of the system can be created following a process

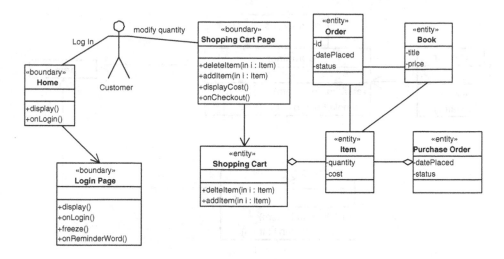

Fig. 5. UML model of an online bookstore

called ICONIX. In ICONIX information which is presented in a browser is stereo-typed as *boundary*. The information that belongs to the business logic is stereotyped as *entity*.

Our aim is to analyse the interaction of the user, through the Web browser, with the business logic of the the online bookstore system modelled by Fig. 5. According to the method described in the previous Section, we have to get rid of the classes that are not related to our aim (i.e. they do not contain any functionality that affects the items in the shopping cart). It is obvious from the model that those classes are the *Home*, the *Login Page*, the *Book*, *Order* and *Purchase Order*. Of course depending on the business logic of the system, the *Purchase Order* might affect the quantity of the items in the shopping cart (i.e. the shopping cart might be emptied after the user has purchased an item), but for reasons of simplicity we are not going to consider this case.

Therefore we are now left with the *Shopping Cart Page*, the *Shopping Cart* and the *Item* classes. We now need to identify which of these classes are used for displaying information on the browser of the user and which for the business logic. However in our case study this is a trivial task as the classes that are used for displaying information to the user are stereotyped as *boundary* and the classes that are part of the business logic are stereotyped as *entity*. Therefore an abstraction of the specification of the functionality of the *Shopping Cart Page* will be used as the specification of the functionality of the *Container*. Similarly an abstraction of the specification of the functionality of the *Shopping Cart* will be used as the specification of the functionality of the *ShoppingCart*. The *Items* are the *Data* the browser exchanges with the business logic. However even from those classes we just need the functionality that changes the contents of the shopping cart. Therefore we can safely get rid of some of the operations of those classes, such as the *displayCost()* and *onCheckout()* of the *Shopping Cart Page* class.

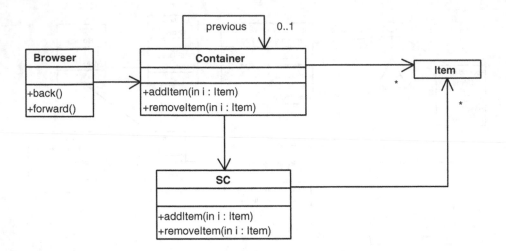

Fig. 6. Abstract Description of Interaction: version 1

Following this reasoning, which is just a practical application of the method described in the previous Section, we end up with the model of Fig. 6.

For practical reasons we had to refactor the model of Fig. 6. As OCL is a language used purely for the specification of systems, it does not allow the specification of an operation to "call" another operation that is not a query operation. A query operation is an operation that does not change the state of the system during its evaluation (e.g. an accessor to an attribute). [16, p. 5] This means that we are not allowed to "call" the *addItem* operation of the *ShoppingCart* from within the *addItem* opeartion of the *Container*, since the former changes the state of the system during its evaluation, by adding one item to the *Shopping-Cart*. In order to overcome this constraint and for reasons of simplicity in the model, we have moved the specification of the functionality of the operations of the *Container* to the *Browser* class. We also consider a smooth communication channel between the browser and the Web server. This enables us to also move the specification of the *addItem* and *removeItem* of the *Shopping Cart* to the *loadItem* and *removeItem* methods of the *Browser* respectively. This change to the ADI does not affect the model of the functionality of the system and the altered model that will be used for the analysis of the system is depicted in Fig. 7.

The *Browser* is related to a *Container*, which represents the Web page the *Browser* displays. We are only interested in the items the user can buy from the Web page. In the model those items are depicted with the *cHasItems* relation. Those are the items in the shopping cart the user sees on his/her Web browser. The *Browser* is also related with the *SC*, which is the shopping cart. The *SC* represents the information held on the server regarding the items the user has added in the shopping cart. The *SC*, like the *Container*, is related to zero or more *Items*.

The *Browser* is a class that represents the Web browser the user uses to access the Web site. The *Browser* class has three operations. The *loadItem* contains the

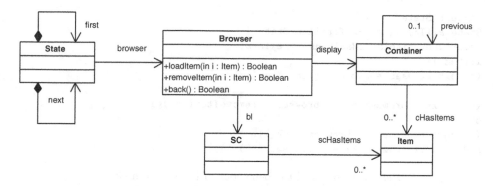

Fig. 7. Abstract Description of Interaction

specification that describes the functionality of the system when the user adds an item, i to the shopping cart. More specifically the *loadItem* operation adds the item to the collection of items the *Container* displays to the user as the shopping cart and also adds it to the collection of items of the shopping cart that the server holds for that session. It also causes a new *Container* to be displayed and the old *Container* is set to be the *previous* of the currently displayed *Container*. In principle this action adds the previously displayed Web page to the Web browser history. The *removeItem* similarly contains the specification for the functionality of the system when the user removes an item i from the shopping cart. The invocation of the *removeItem* operation removes the item from the shopping cart the browser displays, adds the page being displayed to the browser history and invokes a communication with the Web server shopping cart informing it that the item has been removed. The *back()* operation specifies the functionality of the system, when the back button of the *Browser* is pressed. In particular it causes the *previous Container* to be displayed, if any exists. Figure 8 depicts the OCL specification of the *back* operation. It is important to note that the use of the back button in any Web browser invokes the previous request sent to the server and also uses cached information locally.

```
context Browser::back () pre: self.display.previous -> size > 0
post: self.display = self@pre.display@pre.previous@pre
```

Fig. 8. Behaviour of "back" button via OCL

State is a reserved class in UML2Alloy. Like any other class, UML2Alloy transforms the UML class *State* to an Alloy Signature with the same name. However if the *State* class exists in a model UML2Alloy makes use of the polymorphic ordering module distributed with the Alloy Analyzer, which provides support for ordered sets. This is the standard way to achieve process modelling in Alloy [28].

There is also an OCL expression related to the *State* class that depicts the initial state of the system. In that state the shopping cart of the *Container* of

```
context State
State.allInstances -> forAll(s:State |
(s.browser.display.cHasItems -> exists(
i:Item |(
(s.next.browser = s.browser.loadItem(i))
or
(s . next . browser = s . browser . removeItem( i ) )
or
((s.next.browser = s.browser.back())
and (s.next.browser.bl = s.browser.bl ))))))
```

Fig. 9. A portion if the behaviour of the model in OCL

the *Browser* does not display any items and the information about the shopping cart that is held on the server does not have any items as well.

The behaviour of the model is depicted by the OCL statement of Fig. 9. The statement defines that for all ($\forall$) States *s* there exists ($\exists$) at least one item *i* in the model so that the next State *s'* can be produced from the previous if either the user adds an item to the shopping cart (the *loadItem* operation) or removes an item (the *removeItem* operation) , or the "back" button of the browser is pressed (the *back()* opeartion). In that case as explained before the interaction with the server does not cause the information about the shopping cart that is held on the server to change as depicted by the statement $s.next.browser.bl = s.browser.bl$.

4.1 Produced Alloy Model

Figure 10 depicts the corresponding Alloy model for the OCL statement of Fig. 9. Naturally, *forAll* and *exists* of OCL are mapped to *all* and *some*. Moreover, the subsequent state of *s*, i.e. *s.next*, is mapped into the state s' : $ord/next(s)$. However, automated transformation from OCL to Alloy is far from trivial. In OCL, the invocation of an operation is achieved when navigating to the class that owns the operation, and then "calling" the operation. In contrast, Alloy predicates and functions are visible to the whole model. Therefore, during the transformation all OCL statements that invoke operations from another class had to be tailored so as to translate only the part that calls the operation. It can also be noted that more parameters have been added to the *loadItem*, *removeItem* and *back()* operations. This is the usual pattern of specifying pre and post conditions in the Alloy language. For further details regarding the transformation from OCL to Alloy, we refer the reader to [19].

```
all s: State ,s':ord/next(s)| some i:Item |
(loadItem(s.browser,s'.browser,i)) ||
(removeItem(s.browser,s'.browser,i)) || (back(s.browser,s'.browser)
  &&
(s'.browser.bl=s.browser . bl) )
```

Fig. 10. Alloy model of the behaviour

4.2   Results of the Analysis

A major requirement of the model depicted by Fig. 7 is to guarantee the integrity of the system by ensuring that the contents of the shopping cart and the list of items on the browser are identical. This can be expressed by the Alloy *assertion* of Fig. 11. Using Alloy Analyzer we can see that the assertion fails. In fact, setting

```
all s: State | s.browser.display.cHasItems = s.browser.bl.scHasItems
```

Fig. 11. Alloy assertion for checking shopping cart against the displayed items

the Alloy *scope* to three, results in a counterexample, which means, there is at least one instance in three evolutions of the system where the items listed in the browser window differ from the items in the shopping cart.

Using Alloy Analyzer the modeller can see not only the instance that violates the assertion, but also all of the traces in the evolution of the system that lead to the violation of the assertion. That way it is easier to locate the inconsistency in the model. The steps to reproduce the bug according to our analysis are the following:

Step 1. The shopping cart of the user is empty and the user browses the Web site.
Step 2. The user adds an item *Item1* to the shopping cart.
Step 3. The user decides that he does not want to buy *Item1* after all, but instead of deleting it from the shopping cart he presses the "back" button to return to the previous shopping cart which is empty.

Comparing the result of our analysis with the motivating observation of the paper [11], we can notice that the bug can occur following a different trace from the one described in [11], but again it involves the use of the "back" button. To remove such bugs, [11] presents a set of solutions. Analysing such solutions is outside of the scope of the paper. However, our method can equally be used to conduct such analysis.

5   Related and Future Work

Because of the state explosion problem [23] and undecidability issues, it is not possible to fully analyse large systems, such as enterprise Web applications. A method to overcome this problem is to either partially analyse the system, focusing on different aspects of the system every time or to abstract the model that represents it. Using this approach we have decided to focus on the analysis of the ADI, an abstract view of the part of model of the system that depicts the interaction between the user and the business logic. Such analysis increases our confidence of the correct functionality of the system. We are currently working on methods of creating the ADI via semi-automated methods, using refactoring methods [26].

A highly promising direction is to adopt form-based approach [29]. *Form-charts* as a formalism developed for the modelling of form-oriented applications is ideal for capturing the interaction of the user interface with the business logic. As a result, it might be possible to use MDA transformations to create a suitable formchart from which the ADI can be inferred. However, this remains a subject for future work.

6   Conclusions

This paper aids to the analysis of enterprise Web applications. The method adopted draws on the Model Driven Architecture. The Platform Independent Model of systems can be used to create the ADI model, an abstraction of the interaction between the browser and the business logic of the system. In order to analyse the ADI, we apply a further MDA transformation and create a corresponding Alloy model. The paper demonstrates that analysing the ADI, it is possible to identify a group of bugs, such as the Amazon bug [11]. Finally the approach presented in the paper is explained via an example of an e-commerce system.

References

1. Fowler, K.: Mission-critical and safety-critical development. IEEE journal of Instrumentation & Measurement Magazine **7** (2004) 52– 59
2. de Alfaro, L.: Model checking the world wide web. In: Computer Aided Verification, 13th International Conference, CAV 2001, Paris, France, July 18-22, 2001, Proceedings. Volume 2102 of Lecture Notes in Computer Science. (2001) 337–349
3. Haydar, M., Petrenko, A., Sahraoui, H.A.: Formal verification of web applications modeled by communicating automata. In: Proceeding of Formal Techniques for Networked and Distributed Systems - FORTE 2004, 24th IFIP WG 6.1 International Conference, Madrid Spain, September 27-30, 2004. Volume 3235 of Lecture Notes in Computer Science. (2004) 115–132
4. Stotts, D., Navon, J.: Model checking cobweb protocols for verification of html frames behavior. In: Model checking cobweb protocols for verification of HTML frames behavior. (2002) 182 –190
5. MDA: Model Driven Architecture website: http://www.omg.org/mda
6. Frankel, D.S.: Model Driven Architecture: Applying MDA to Enterprise Computing. Wiley Publishing, Indianapolis, Indiana (2003)
7. Kleppe, A., Warmer, J., Bast, W.: MDA Explained: The Model Driven Architecture - Practice and Promise. The Addison-Wesley Object Technology Series. Addison-Wesley (2003)
8. Jackson, D.: Alloy 3.0 Reference Manual (May 2004) Software Design Group, MIT Lab for Computer Science, http://alloy.mit.edu/beta/reference-manual.pdf.
9. Jackson, D.: Alloy: a lightweight object modelling notation. ACM Transactions on Software Engineering and Methodology (TOSEM) **11** (2002) 256–290
10. W3C: W3C website: http://www.w3.org/

11. Baresi, L., Denaro, G., Mainetti, L., Paolini, P.: Assertions to better specify the amazon bug. In: SEKE '02: Proceedings of the 14th international conference on Software engineering and knowledge engineering, New York, NY, USA, ACM Press (2002) 585–592

12. Licata, D.R., Krishnamurthi, S.: Verifying interactive web progams. In: 19th IEEE International Conference on Automated Software Engineering (ASE 2004), Linz, Austria, IEEE Press (2004) 164–173

13. Interactive Objects: Archstyler website: http://www.interactive-objects.com/

14. AndroMDA: AndroMDA website: http://www.andromda.org/

15. Object Management Group: UML 2.0 Superstructure Final Adopted Specification. Document id: ptc/03-08-02. http://www.omg.org/docs/ptc/03-08-02.pdf.

16. Object Management Group: UML 2.0 OCL Final Adopted Specification. Document id: ptc/03-10-14. http://www.omg.org/cgi-bin/doc?ptc/2003-10-14.

17. Alloy Analyzer: Alloy Analyzer website: http://alloy.mit.edu/

18. UML2Alloy: http://www.cs.bham.ac.uk/$\sim$bxb/UML2Alloy.php

19. Bordbar, B., Anastasakis, K.: UML2Alloy: A tool for lightweight modelling of Discrete Event Systems. In Guimarães, N., Isaías, P., eds.: IADIS International Conference in Applied Computing 2005. Volume 1., Algarve, Portugal, IADIS Press (2005) 209–216

20. Object Managemenet Group (OMG): OMG website: http://www.omg.org

21. Object Management Group: Meta Object Facility (MOF) 2.0 Core Specification. Document Id: ptc/03-10-04. http://www.omg.org/cgi-bin/apps/do_doc?ptc/03-10-04.pdf

22. Jackson, D.: Automating first-order relational logic. In: SIGSOFT '00/FSE-8: Proceedings of the 8th ACM SIGSOFT international symposium on Foundations of software engineering, New York, NY, USA, ACM Press (2000) 130–139

23. Valmari, A.: The state explosion problem. In: Lectures on Petri Nets I: Basic Models, Advances in Petri Nets, the volumes are based on the Advanced Course on Petri Nets. Volume 1492 of LNCS., London, UK, Springer-Verlag (1998) 429–528

24. ArgoUML: ArgoUML website: http://argouml.tigris.org/

25. Object Management Group: UML 2.0 Diagram Interchange Final Adopted Specification. Document Id:ptc/03-09-01. http://www.omg.org.

26. Fowler, M., Beck, K., Brant, J., Opdyke, W., Roberts, D.: Refactoring: improving the design of existing code. Addison-Wesley, Boston, MA, USA (1999)

27. Rosenberg, D., Scott, K.: Applying Use Case Driven Object Modeling with UML: An Annotated E-Commerce Example. Addison-Wesley Object Technology Series. Addison-Wesley (2001)

28. Wallace, C.: Using Alloy in process modelling. Information and Software Technology **45** (2003) 1031–1043

29. Draheim, D., Weber, G.: Form-Oriented Analysis: A New Methodology to Model Form-Based Applications. Springer-Verlag, Berlin, Germany (2005)

A Message Exchange Architecture for Modern E-Commerce

Barry Dowdeswell[1] and Christof Lutteroth[2]

[1] AARN Innovation Limited,
P.O.Box 82-171, Highland Park, Auckland, New Zealand
barry@aarn.biz
[2] Department of Computer Science, The University of Auckland,
38 Princes Street, Auckland 1020, New Zealand
lutteroth@cs.auckland.ac.nz

Abstract. This paper describes the EDIS business messaging architecture, which is a modern, lightweight system that is used in numerous companies. It explains the requirements for such a system, the problematic issues that have to be dealt with, and also some aspects of the wider context of e-commerce. Furthermore, it compares the presented architecture to similar systems like, for example, MS BizTalk and discusses related research on enterprise architecture.

1 Introduction

In the business world, computers have been used since the 50's and have become an important tool for modern business. All the large enterprises rely heavily on systems for enterprise resource planning (ERP) which integrate and automate many of their administrative tasks. In the 90's the focus of enterprise computing shifted to the Internet, and the idea to use the net in order to make business with customers (B2C) ended in heavy losses for many investors and companies. In the last years another aspect has come to general attention: computer-supported business between businesses (B2B). Again, the Internet is supposed to bring revolutionary changes to the enterprise world, and this alleged revolution is heralded by a plethora of new standards trying make their way into the enterprise.

When looking at these things from a scientific perspective, it is extremely important to distinguish between fact and hype, between what technologies are and what people want them to be. For all what it seems, computer supported B2B is an old concept that dates back to the 80's. At that time, the main standards defining the format of business messages were that of electronic data interchange (EDI) [8], and the infrastructure on which these messages were transported were value-added networks (VANs). Although it may seem, with the emergence of XML-based data formats and the web services technology [15], that EDI is outdated, one has to acknowledge that the overwhelming majority of B2B traffic is still done using the old standards. These technologies worked successfully for twenty years now, while most new standards have still to prove themselves. And

D. Draheim and G. Weber (Eds.): TEAA 2005, LNCS 3888, pp. 56–70, 2006.

no matter how mature new standards will turn out to be, the old standards will continue to be used for quite some years to come.

The system described in this paper is one for business message exchange. It was developed from the mid-nineties onward to be an easily deployable B2B solution that can be adjusted to the changing needs of a company. Its creators have been in the e-commerce business since it began in the 80's, and as a consequence the system supports old standards for message transport and encoding as well as new ones and can interface to different ERP systems. It is extensible and designed with the possibility of future change in mind.

2 Requirements for Modern B2B

Before we discuss the architecture of the EDIS B2B system, we would like to point out the requirements that a modern B2B system has to satisfy. These requirements have changed, since the new wave of B2B standards brings up new maturity and compatibility issues. Standards for electronic B2B have become a strategic factor, which means that decisions about it have to be considered carefully.

First of all, it is not always possible for a company to choose their B2B standard themselves. Many companies depend on trade relationships with bigger business partners, and if such a business partner decides to change its e-commerce system, might very well expect its smaller partners to adjust to it. This makes *flexibility* of a system a basic requirement, especially in today's world where many changes are just about to occur. As we can see, for example, in [14], the strategies with which companies adopt new B2B technologies can differ significantly. The evolving nature of electronic B2B and the steady change that takes place has been subject to many studies, e.g., the one described in [9]. It is important to note that we usually need not just a single standard for B2B message exchange: there exist, for example, different standards for message encoding and message transport, respectively, and those standards can be combined in many different ways. To sum up, a flexible B2B system has to support different standards for different tasks, and it should be possible to combine them in different ways.

Another aspect of flexibility concerns the workflow that a B2B system supports. This workflow, which might, for example, define what happens when a system error occurs, may also be subject to steady change. Therefore, it must not only be possible to configure the technological behaviour of the system, but it must also be possible to change the way the system reacts to different circumstances that may occur.

Different companies often have different ERP systems. Some companies even have their own particular one. Whatever the ERP system is that a company uses, a good message exchange system has to be able to interface to any of them. Since the interface to the ERP system can be a very proprietary one, it may be necessary to create a customized adapter component. A good B2B system will support a developer in this task.

In contrast to B2C, B2B is usually not dealing with huge loads of transactions. Consequently, performance is not as important as in B2C. Whereas in B2C we usually do not expect a single business transactions to have a particularly high value, but rather expect many transactions with relatively small value, the value of a B2B transaction can be extremely high. A flawed B2B transaction can cause immense costs. Therefore we have to make sure that erroneous messages are singled out, either automatically or manually. In order to perform such error checking, the system needs to have some knowledge about the business logic; and since business logic varies from company to company, it must be possible to configure it as easily as possible. For correct business messages manual translation does not make sense: it is a tiring task and that makes it particularly error prone. However, if an erroneous message is detected, human intervention is an absolute necessity. For resolving errors, human intelligence is irreplaceable, and trying to resolve errors automatically would be too high a risk. Nevertheless, a good B2B system should support the workflow of *error handling* done by humans.

A B2B system has to offer high *reliability*. If messages get lost or corrupted, this can have disastrous consequences for the supply chain of a business. Thus, such a system has to rely on mature technology, like, for example, a good database management system. Only if a persistent log is kept, the system can be brought back into a consistent state after failure. Since such a system naturally involves many business partners, errors might not necessarily occur just in the local system, but in any system involved. A B2B system has to work correctly even if other's systems fail, and must also handle and resolve errors created by others. It has to be *fail operational*, i.e., remain in an operational state even when an error occurs. Whatever happens, the system has to log every major system event, like incoming and outgoing messages, message translation and possible failures. Only like this a system can, for example, detect when duplicate messages are received and prevent duplicate processing. A very important issue related to reliability is *availability*. While it may be tolerable in B2C when a service is temporarily unavailable, this is totally unacceptable for a business. In B2C this may cost a couple of small successful trades, but in B2B this can be existential.

Last but not least, a B2B system has to guarantee *security*. This has different aspects: first of all, mechanisms like digital certificates and signatures have to make sure that all the sender of each message is authentified. Once *authentification* is done, we can use it in order to prevent unauthorized messages from being processed, i.e., ensure *access control*. Usually we also do not want others to get to know the content of the business messages, so we have to apply *encryption* to make them unreadable to others. Finally, a business partner might want a unforgeable receipt for the reception and/or processing of a message, which establishes a property called *non-repudiation*, i.e., the business partner at the other end cannot repudiate the reception and/or processing of the message.

3   The EDIS Architecture

Figure 1 shows an overview of the system's architecture. As we can see, the system consists of different modules, some of which form groups that take care of a particular aspect of the system's functionality. On the left side of the figure we have different modules for handling the transport of in- and outgoing message with different protocols. On the right of the figure we have different modules for the translation of messages, which handle the data flow between message queue and ERP system. The message queue is the central data structure of the messaging system, with the transport protocol modules storing and retrieving messages from it.

Many of the system's modules are written in an interpreted scripting language which is largely equivalent to MS Visual Basic. Some of the transport protocol modules and all of the translation modules are implemented as scripts. This has the advantage that these modules are very easy to program, to deploy and to debug. The scripting language offers a high level of abstraction through a comprehensive framework of library functions. It eliminates the need for compilation to a low-level representation, which makes it platform independent. Scripts are controlled by the interpreter and sufficiently isolated from the rest of the system; this makes it possible to ensure safety of execution and control a script's capabilities, i.e., the functions of the system it is allowed to use, making execution also secure. The clean abstract interface of the interpreter and its inherent capacity to control the execution flow of a script make debugging easier. Although interpretation is naturally slower than the execution of compiled code this is, as we have discussed in Sect. 2, not a problematic issue.

Its scripting capabilities make the system highly customisable, since scripts allow the developer to freely develop translation and communications functions

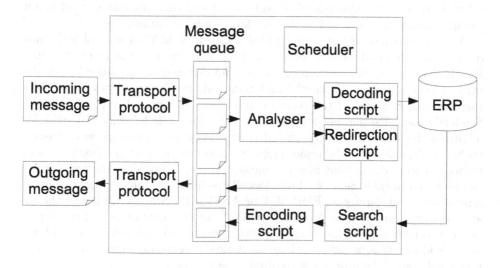

Fig. 1. Overview of the EDIS system

specific to their needs. Note, however, that this flexibility does not infringe the system's integrity: the system has a mature, "closed" core and library that ensures the scripts operate in an consistent and safe environment. While end-users who are developers have full access to the script source, they cannot modify the core modules such as, e.g., the scheduler, the AS2 protocol implementation or the EDIFACT library parsing routines.

All scripts are, directly or indirectly, activated by the scheduler of the system. This module allows it to start scripts at regular time intervals. The analyser module collects elementary data about a message and then delegates the its processing to an appropriate translation script. In the following sections we will describe all of these parts in detail.

3.1   The Message Queue

The message queue is the central data structure in the system. Whatever message passes through the system will be archived in the message queue. It is implemented on a relational database, which controls the access to it by all the other system parts and makes sure that the data remains in a consistent state. Since the message queue is such an important part of the system, we want to cover it in more detail and explain how its relational schema looks like.

Before a message is sent it is usually put into an electronic envelope. Such envelopes can hold multiple messages that are sent to a business partner in a single delivery. The message queue keeps track of envelopes as well as of newly created messages that are not enveloped yet. For each envelope the system has to keep track of the different messages embedded in it. This is achieved with two tables, Queue and QueueXref, which are illustrated at the top of Fig. 2. Table Queue contains all the envelopes and unenveloped messages currently stored in the system, together with fields that explicitly describe some of their fundamental properties. Table QueueXref keeps track of and contains information about the messages that are stored in the envelopes of table Queue.

Let us first consider the records of table Queue: field MsgData holds the raw data of an individual message or an envelope as it was received or created in a BLOB. Field EDI_ref is a running integer number and the primary key of the table. Fields SenderID, PartnerID and ServideID are foreign keys to the tables Partners and Services. If the record contains a message and not an envelope, SenderID identifies the message's sender, otherwise it is left blank. PartnerID identifies the business partner an individual message or envelope is addressed to. ServiceID references the remote service a message or envelope should be sent to; more information about how to transfer data to a particular remote service can be found in table Services. Field DocuType identifies the message format of a message or envelope, e.g., EDIFACT or ANSI X.12. Naturally, all messages in an envelope share the same format. DocuDir contains the direction of envelopes, i.e., if it is inbound and has been received or outbound and will be or has been sent. Field DocuStatus indicates if an entry needs processing or has already been processed, and if the processing resulted in any error.

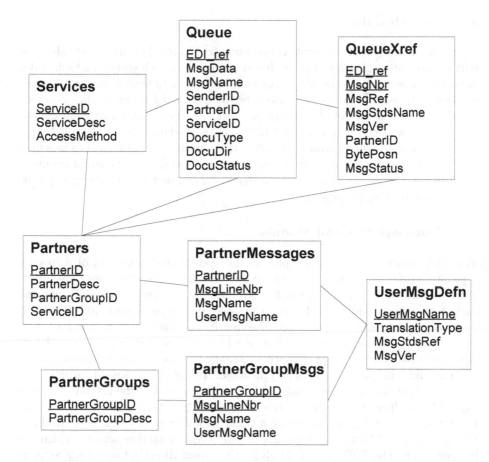

Fig. 2. General structure of the EDIS data model

Table QueueXref contains data about all messages that are stored in one of Queue's envelopes. It also contains field EDI_ref, which refers to an envelope in Queue, and a field MsgNbr, which is the running number of the respective message within that envelope. Together, EDI_ref and MsgNbr form the primary key of the table. MsgRef contains a message reference number that is used to uniquely identify messages of a particular business partner, which is important for detecting duplicates. It helps to make message reception idempotent, i.e., makes sure that messages which are received twice are only processed once. MsgStdsName and MsgVer contain information about the standard and the version of the standard the message adheres to. PartnerID is a foreign key to table Partners and identifies the message's creator. Since each message in QueueXref is embedded in the BLOB field MsgData of an entry of Queue, we also keep track of the starting position BytePosn of each message within the BLOB. Field MsgStatus indicates whether this message has not been or has already been decoded, and if any errors occurred during the decoding process.

3.2   The Scheduler

Many of the scripts of the system are executed in regular time intervals. The part of the system that manages such time events is the scheduler. The scheduler organizes time events in so-called process lines that are specified in the following manner: it is possible to set the days of the week on which an event should occur, the time of day the event should first be sent, the time of day the event can be sent at last, and the frequency in which the event should be rescheduled after having been sent. These parameters allow it to specify the time pattern in which e-commerce usually takes place. All data about scheduling and current events is available in the system's relational database and can be read by other programs, e.g., for monitoring purposes.

3.3   Transport Protocol Modules

Transport protocol modules are part of the system that take care of a specific type of message transportation. As we have mentioned earlier there are different standards and non-standards for the different functions of a B2B message exchange system, and a good system has to be able to support all of them if required. An important business partner might just adopt a new standard, and the system has to adjust to this. This is why the transport subsystem of EDIS has a modular structure that decouples message transportation from other parts.

A module can support sending of messages, reception, or both. It is activated by a system event, which is usually either a timer signal or the arrival of a message. The sending of messages is always triggered by a timer signal, whereas the reception can be either triggered by a timer signal or message arrival. Modules that are triggered by timer signals are usually implemented as scripts, which are interpreted by the B2B system. Modules that react directly to message arrivals are usually implemented as server extensions to, for example, the MS Internet Information Server (IIS). This diversity is necessary in order to deal with the different ways a message can be sent and received, of which we will describe a few.

One way to transport messages is to simply use the email infrastructure. Email communication can be secured, for example, by combining it with transport layer security (TLS), and authentification can be established by using digital signing as described in the S/MIME standard. The transport protocol module is triggered by a timer signal in regular intervals, and each time the module is started, it connects to the respective mail server, retrieves the new messages, removes the mail specific data from them and stores them into the message queue. The messages are marked as unprocessed inbound messages. Besides for retrieving messages form a mail server, the module also checks the message queue for outbound messages that are to be sent to business partners that use email as transport protocol. Once these messages have been delivered to the respective mail server, they are marked as sent. One of the advantages of this architecture is that existing email infrastructure can be used. Rather than having to implement its own mail server, the system can interface to existing ones and thereby make the actual message transport independent of other tasks particular to B2B.

A transport module similar to the one that uses email transfers the messages to and from a business partner's file system using the file transfer protocol (FTP). This protocol can be secured, for example, by tunnelling it over the secure shell protocol. The module is executed in regular time intervals, looks for new files on a business partner's file system and for new messages in the message queue, performs the appropriate file transfer operations and updates the message queue. Although FTP is a standardized protocol, the exact transport process via FTP usually varies between business partners: business partners have their own rules for the file names and file locations particular message types have to be stored to. Consequently, such kind of modules have to be adjustable. This is achieved through the relatively high abstraction level of the scripting language in which these modules are written. Again, the system profits from the fact that it can use any FTP server for message transport.

The module for handling inbound AS2 communication [3] is an example for a module that is executed on arrival of a message. AS2, short for application statement 2, is a business message transport standard proposed by the IETF. It encapsulates message data in a MIME or S/MIME envelope and sends it via HTTP. This is why the AS2 reception module is implemented as a MS IIS HTTP handler. Whenever an AS2 message arrives, the handler is called and stores the received data into the message queue. Since the message queue is implemented on a transactional database management system, it does not matter how many such handlers are working concurrently. The database management system takes care of all the concurrency issues.

Modules handling outbound communication can access the system's relational database in order to get the parameters that are need to send a message. Table Services, which is illustrated in the top left corner of the data model in Fig. 2, contains an entry for each remote service a message can be send to. Field ServiceID is the table's primary key and is used to associate the service with any message in table Queue that should be send to it. ServiceDesc describes each of the available services. Field AccessMethod and other fields, which we will not mention further, provide the necessary technical details for sending messages to the respective service provider.

3.4   Message Analysis

In regular time intervals the analysis module is run. It searches the message queue for incoming envelopes that have not been processed yet. The analysis module parses each message in such an envelope and determines what format the messages are stored in and if the messages are well-formed. If a message is well-formed, some of its basic properties are extracted, like its sender, its receiver, the message type, e.g, if it is an invoice or purchase order, and its unique reference number. These data are used in order to create a record in table QueueXref that describes the respective message of the envelope. In order to decode a message and take appropriate action, we have to make use of the data about our business partners and the messages they send that is stored in the system's data base. The tables involved here are illustrated in the bottom part of Fig. 2.

Once a message has been analysed we need to start a script that handles its further processing. Each kind of message is handled by a particular script, which, in the case of incoming messages, either decodes the message or redirects it. Decoding scripts and redirection scripts are described in Sects. 3.5 and 3.8, respectively. For each message kind there is a record in table UserMsgDefn, which contains a reference to the script that should be used. In field TranslationType this record contains the type of the script, e.g., encoding or decoding, and in fields MsgStdsRef and MsgVer the type of the processed message is described.

For choosing the right script for an incoming message, we use its type and its sender, both of which have been extracted already. Table Partners contains an entry for each business partner messages are sent to or received from. Each business partner supports a well-defined set of message kinds that they can send or receive. The data model allows us to map a type and a sender, which has an entry in partners, unambiguously to a script. One way to define this mapping is to modify table PartnerMessages, which can arbitrarily associate entries in table Partners with entries in table UserMsgDefn. Field PartnerID is a foreign key to table partners; field UserMsgName is a foreign key to table UserMsgDefn. The fields PartnerID and MsgLineNbr form the primary key of the table, with MsgLineNbr being a running number for all the kinds of messages a respective business partner supports.

It would be possible to link all business partners with the message kinds they support using table PartnerMessages. However, usually there are groups of business partners which communicate amongst themselves using a common standard and therefore use the same set of message kinds. In order to simplify the relation between partners and message kinds and make them easier to maintain, the data model supports this concept of groups of business partners by providing tables PartnerGroups and PartnerGroupMsgs. Field PartnerGroupID of table Partners is a foreign key to table PartnerGroups, which contains a description of every group of business partners. It allows to associate a business partner with a group and join groups with entries in table PartnerGroupMsgs. Table PartnerGroupMsgs follows the same pattern as table PartnerMessages, only that UserMsgDefn records are associated with records in PartnerGroups. The advantage of business partner groups is that changes to the message kinds of a group affects all group members, thus preserving compatibility of their communication.

3.5   Decoding Scripts

As we have described in Sect. 3.4, decoding scripts are chosen and executed by the analyser when inbound messages are processed. A decoding script parses a message, extracts all important information and stores this information into the database of an ERP system. In order to perform the translation of messages into ERP records, decoding scripts have to be aware of the message's syntax and semantics as well as the structure of the ERP system's data base. Hence, writing such scripts is not a trivial task, and correctness of such scripts is very important.

A scipt's capabilities, i.e., the operations it is allowed to perform, should be minimal. This way we can avoid many errors and detect some unwanted behaviour. One way to realize this is to configure the interpreter accordingly: it can control the access of the script to other modules while it is running. Another way to restrict access and thereby increase safety is to use the access control mechanism of the ERP system's database: a script should only have write access to those tables that it really needs to modify.

Last but not least, it is very important to handle errors in scripts appropriately. If an error occurs, the error has to be logged and possible modifications that have already been made by the scripts have to be undone. A script has to be *atomic*, i.e., either complete successfully or have no effect at all except on the system's logs. The general structure imposed on the scripts satisfies all these requirements. If a script produces a significant amount of errors, something in the system is most probably wrong. It may be that the script is erroneous, but it may also be that a business partner changed their messages without the system being adjusted to the change. Whatever the reason, such a script will be singled out and put into quarantine, and the errors are automatically reported to the person responsible for the respective kind of message.

3.6 Search Scripts

Search scripts are run by the scheduler in regular time intervals. They search parts of an ERP system's database that contain information which has to be sent to other business partners, like, for example, invoices or purchase orders. For that they run a database query and keep the query results in an ephemeral todo-list, which contains some basic information about every ERP record that is to be sent. When the todo-list is complete, the search script uses the data in the todo-list, like intended message recipient and message type, in order to select a script that can encode the the data into a message. This is analogous to the task of the analyser of selecting a decoding script, which was described in Sect. 3.4, and makes use of the same database tables. Encoding scripts are described in Sect. 3.7. A search script finishes when all todo-list entries have been processed by appropriate encoding scripts.

3.7 Encoding Scripts

An encoding script is activated when a search script finds new data in an ERP database that needs to be sent out of the system. The encoding script is given the location of the ERP data it has to encode, extracts the required information from the ERP database and assembles a new message that is written into the queue. As soon as an appropriate transport protocol module is run by the scheduler, the newly created messages are sent.

In order to keep track of the ERP records which have already been encoded and avoid multiple encoding of the same record, encoding scripts use additional database tables. These tables can either be part of the messaging system's or the ERP system's database. The advantage of keeping them in the messaging system is that ERP and messaging system are decoupled more and the risk of interference between the systems is reduced. The advantage of keeping them in the ERP database is that the search query of a search script, which must only return unsent records, can be executed more efficiently.

Encoding scripts are subject to the same safety requirements as decoding scripts, which were described in Sect. 3.5. The capabilities such a script has have to be adjusted carefully, e.g., the script should only be able to access those parts of the ERP system that are needed. Like decoding scripts, encoding scripts have to behave atomic and must handle and report errors carefully.

3.8   Redirection Scripts

Like decoding scripts, redirection scripts are started by the analyser after a new inbound message has been analysed. However, instead of decoding the message and storing it into an ERP system, the message is decoded and afterwards encoded as a new outbound message. The encoding creates a new entry in the message queue that will be found and sent by one of the transport protocol modules. This makes it possible for the system to act as a hub in a network of business partners. It can mediate and translate the message exchange between business partners who use different messaging standards, thus allowing them to communicate without changing their system.

3.9   Maintenance Scripts

Another category of scripts is that of maintenance scripts. These scripts are usually called by the scheduler in regular time intervals and automatically perform maintenance tasks which are important for the system. A maintenance script might, for example, backup and archive all system data or produce a report on the system's recent activity.

4   Tool Support

Because the creation of translation scripts like encoding and decoding scripts is a skilled task that consumes considerable time when done manually, the messaging system contains an integrated development environment (IDE), EDIS map, that can reduce the development time of such scripts drastically. By automating large parts of the actual decoding and encoding of messages, EDIS map avoids many potential programming errors and makes the development of translation scripts easier and safer. The IDE supports old messaging standards like EDIFACT and ANSI X.12 as well as newer XML-based message standards.

EDIS map facilitates the creation of translation scripts in several ways. It offers a set of templates for standard translation tasks that can be easily modified and adapted according to the business rules of a particular business partner. New message translation scripts can be created by importing sample messages or message schemas. The IDE makes meta information of several target database systems like, for example, MS SQL Server and Borland Interbase, accessible, so that scripts can easier be programmed to use these database systems. The tool integrates documentation of messages and can export documentation about message mappings in human readable form. Furthermore, it can automatically generate documentation suitable for regression testing of scripts.

Rather than dealing with a single monolithic script that does all the work involved in processing a message, we associate code snippets to message segments that merely process the data in the respective message segment. Individual segments of a message can be examined, specified and documented. This approach results in a natural decomposition of the translation process.

EDIS map also contains the usual features of advanced IDEs. It supports automatic formatting and syntax highlighting of code and message data, a context-sensitive help and automatic code completion. Syntax checking is performed and syntax errors are reported immediately; also runtime and compile-time errors are reported within the IDE. The integrated debugger allows to trace the execution of scripts in single steps.

5   Related Work

There exist theoretical models for the description of messaging systems, which can be applied to the B2B context. One such model is described in [4]. It is possible to describe messaging as done by the EDIS system with the data type interchange models delineated in this work. In the terminology of [5], EDIS provides the technological means for data exchange in interorganizational relationships between business partners. It is mainly used for relationships governed by a market, although it is also possible to use it for relationships governed by a hierarchy or a hybrid of both. EDIS is not limited to dyadic or "hub and spoke" type relationships, but can be applied to organization networks as well. It provides all the functions of a B2B engine as described in [1] as well as some additional B2B integration functions, like integration of ERP systems.

There are various B2B systems on the market that offer capabilities similar to those of EDIS. One of them is MS BizTalk [11]. BizTalk offers B2B functionality similar to EDIS, although it intends to perform not only B2B messaging but also enterprise application integration (EAI) and, most of all, business process management (BPM). It has been described, for example, how BizTalk can be used in order to manage B2b contracts electronically [7]. Whereas EDIS focusses on enabling business partners to communicate, BizTalk also tries to define and execute high-level programs, so-called "orchestrations", which are supposed to express business processes. These programs can be edited in a visual form and are equivalent in expressiveness to the programming language BPEL [12], which claims to achieve a higher level of abstraction that is closer to real business processes by focusing on "programming in the large". Regarding the original intention of business process modelling as described, e.g., in [13], it is, however, arguable whether orchestrations can really reach to that level, or if they rather just describe the business logic. Such an approach is not inherently more appropriate than the scripting approach chosen in EDIS. The overall architecture of BizTalk is similar to EDIS: the system contains modules for handling different transport protocols, which are called "adapters", and messages are stored in a central relational database, which is called "message box". A central component, the "orchestration engine", executes and feeds messages into orchestrations according to the message's properties and perform further processing.

A main difference of BizTalk to EDIS is that all messages in the message box are stored in some format based on XML. This can be explained by the point of view that XML inherently provides added value for B2B, as it is also expressed in different academic publications, e.g., [6] and [16], and by Microsoft's current technological strategy. Consequently, incoming and outgoing messages need to be translated to and from XML in so-called "pipelines". For different message formats we need different sets of receiving and sending pipelines. While the usage of XML as a common intermediate format helps to standardise and reduce modules preforming translation tasks and makes it possible to handle message content in a common way, it also introduces the need to translate between different XML formats since XML is not a well-defined message format in itself. Therefore, Biztalk comes with a CASE tool called BizTalk Mapper for creating XSL transformations [18] between different XML schemas. This is slightly similar to EDIS map, but in contrast to BizTalk Mapper, EDIS map supports the translation between essentially different data formats, not just between different flavours of XML, which is a more difficult task.

Another important difference to EDIS is that BizTalk has a very large footprint and depends on various other Microsoft products. Integration with other products may on the one hand provide the user with more functionality and may enrich the way a user can interact with a system, but on the other hand, dependencies between products force customers to spend money on all the required products and binds them to the respective company.

BizTalk, like many other products, make a big point of claiming that they deliver service oriented architecture (SOA) [10]. In general, SOA describes a software architecture for enterprise systems in which components are distributed in a network and can use each other by utilizing a common remote function invocation mechanism. Each component, which is also called a "service", performs a well-defined business task and can be implemented with arbitrary technology as long as it provides the same network interface as the others. When most companies speak about SOA, they refer to the very particular remoting technology of web services, the heart of which is the simple object access protocol (SOAP) [17]. In the context of B2B, web services are just one possible way of many for business partners to communicate; consequently, web services is just one of the transport protocols a B2B system like BizTalk or EDIS can provide in order to fit into a SOA. The software architecture of the BizTalk or EDIS systems themselves is usually not SOA, but rather a structured, component-oriented and non-distributed one. In the case of EDIS, the system consists of modules that mostly interoperate asynchronously using the message queue, which is accessed by SQL. Other commercial systems which follow the trend of SOA and have B2B capabilities similar to EDIS are, for example, IBM WebSphere MQ and Cordys.

There are many studies describing the complexity of the implementation of B2B systems in various companies; see for example [2]. Taking into account past experiences with B2B, it is questionable whether a new B2B software can really revolutionize the way electronic business is done. One should mark that that the ways of electronic business are usually subject to evolutionary – not revolutionary – change.

6 Conclusion

We described the EDIS B2B messaging system, its overall architecture and the design of its important components like, for example, the scheduler, the message analyser and the message queue. We also described EDIS map, which is a CASE tool for creating translation scripts for EDIS. Besides pointing out the general requirements of a B2B system, we also compared EDIS to other popular systems with B2B messaging capabilities. While many other products claim to have a significant impact on a business by offering business process engines and promoting service oriented architecture, EDIS is not intended to promote or change any architectural principles. It rather makes a point of not being prescriptive and enable different companies to communicate without interfering with their business processes.

References

1. Christoph Bussler. The role of B2B engines in B2B integration architectures. *SIGMOD Rec.*, 31(1):67–72, 2002.
2. Caroline Chan and Paula M.C. Swatman. Management and business issues for B2B eCommerce implementation. In *Proceedings of the 35th Annual Hawaii International Conference on System Sciences*. IEEE Press, January 2002.
3. D. Moberg and R. Drummond. RFC4130: MIME-Based Secure Peer-to-Peer Business Data Interchange Using HTTP, Applicability Statement 2 (AS2). RFC, July 2005.
4. Dirk Draheim and Gerald Weber. *Form-Oriented Analysis - A New Methodology to Model Form-Based Applications*. Springer, October 2004.
5. Wafa Elgarah, Natalia Falaleeva, Carol C. Saunders, Virginia Ilie, J. T. Shim, and James. F. Courtney. Data exchange in interorganizational relationships: review through multiple conceptual lenses. *SIGMIS Database*, 36(1):8–29, 2005.
6. Wilhelm Hasselbring and Hans Weigand. Languages for Electronic Business Communication: State of the Art. *Industrial Management & Data Systems*, 101(5): 217–226, 2001.
7. Charles Herring and Zoran Milosevic. Implementing B2B Contracts Using BizTalk. In *Proceedings of the 34th Annual Hawaii International Conference on System Sciences*. IEEE Press, January 2001.
8. Paul Kimberley. *Electronic Data Interchange*. McGraw Hill, 1991.
9. Chang E. Koh and Kyungdoo Nam. Business use of the Internet: A longitudinal study from a value chain perspective. *Industrial Management & Data Systems*, 105(1):82–95, January 2005.
10. Mircosoft Inc. BizTalk Server 2004 Architecture. Whitepaper, December 2003.

11. Mircosoft Inc. Understanding BizTalk Server 2004. Technical Article, February 2004.
12. Organization for the Advancement of Structured Information Standards. Web Services Business Process Execution Language Version 2.0. Working Draft, May 2005.
13. August-Wilhelm Scheer. *Aris: Business Process Modeling*. Springer, 2000.
14. Arie Segev, Jaana Porra, and Malu Roldan. Internet-based EDI strategy. *Decision Support Systems*, 21(3):157–170, 1997.
15. Aaron E Walsh. *UDDI, SOAP, and WSDL: The Web Services Specification Reference Book*. Pearson Education, April 2002.
16. Tim Weitzel, Peter Buxmann, and Falk von Westarp. A Communication Architecture for the Digital Economy - 21st Century EDI. In *Proceedings of the 33th Annual Hawaii International Conference on System Sciences*. IEEE Press, January 2000.
17. World Wide Web Consortium. SOAP Version 1.2. Recommendation, June 2003.
18. World Wide Web Consortium. XSL Transformations (XSLT) Version 2.0. Working Draft, April 2005.

Architecture for Distributed ERP Systems

Lars Frank

Department of Informatics, Copenhagen Business School, Howitzvej 60,
DK-2000 Frederiksberg, Denmark
Phone: +45 38 15 2400; Fax: +45 38152401
frank@CBS.DK

Abstract. In a distributed ERP (Enterprise Resource Planning) system, the different local ERP systems are integrated in such a way that each local system can use the resources/stocks managed by the other local ERP systems. Businesses with branch offices may derive great benefits from such systems. In theory, such a system can be built by using a distributed DBMS (Data Base Management System). However, distributed DBMSs are not used in practice as e.g. performance and local autonomy are low. In distributed databases with relaxed ACID properties (Atomicity, Consistency, Isolation, and Durability), it is possible to optimize performance, local autonomy, and availability by using short duration locking. In such systems, data is not locked across locations, i.e. data is not locked across a dialog with a user, and replicated data must be updated asynchronously. In this paper, we will describe how it is possible to design a distributed ERP system by using databases with relaxed ACID properties. The techniques described are general in the sense that most package software run on separate computers may be integrated by using the same methods. The author has cooperated with one of the major ERP software companies in analyzing how the company can design such a distributed version of their ERP system.

1 Introduction

The *countermeasure transaction model* [1] is the extended transaction model used in this paper to implement relaxed ACID properties. In this model, *countermeasures* [1] are used against the isolation anomalies that may occur when transactions are executed without or with reduced isolation against concurrent transactions. The relaxed ACID properties are used to improve performance and availability. In this paper, different replication designs are used to enhance local autonomy and further improve performance and availability. The major disadvantages of data replication are the additional costs of updating replicated data and the problems related to managing the consistency of the replicated data. However, when replicated data is updated asynchronously, it is normally possible to use the same countermeasures against isolation anomalies and consistency problems in the replicated data.

To implement countermeasures against lack of consistency and isolation may be expensive. Therefore, the techniques described are most attractive to software companies developing package software such as ERP systems, as the development costs may be shared with many buyers.

D. Draheim and G. Weber (Eds.): TEAA 2005, LNCS 3888, pp. 71–83, 2006.
© Springer-Verlag Berlin Heidelberg 2006

The paper is organized as follows: Sect. 2 will describe how relaxed ACID properties may be implemented by using an extended transaction model. Sect. 3 will describe and evaluate the replication designs used in this paper. Sect. 4 will integrate the extended transaction model described in Sect. 2 with the replication designs described in Sect. 3 to design a distributed ERP system optimized for high performance, high availability, and local autonomy. Related work will be discussed in Sect. 5. Concluding remarks and future research will be presented in Sect 6.

2   The Transaction Model

In this section, we will describe the *countermeasure transaction model* [1] where *global transactions* [14] may access data located in more than one local database. This is important in distributed ERP systems where the stocks are managed by local ERP systems running in different locations.

In the countermeasure transaction model, a global transaction has a *root transaction* (client transaction) and several single site *subtransactions* (server transactions) that may be nested, i.e. a subtransaction may be a *parent transaction* for other subtransactions. Data is accessed through subtransactions that either are an execution of a *stored procedure,* which automatically returns control to the parent transaction, or an execution of a *stored program* that does not return control to the parent transaction. Subtransactions are invoked by either RPC or UPs as described in the following:

Remote Procedure Call (RPC)
A RPC functions as a remote procedure call or submission of a SQL query. RPCs have the following properties, which are important from a performance and an atomicity point of view:

- If a parent transaction executes several RPCs, the corresponding stored procedures are executed one at a time.
- A stored procedure or SQL submission has only local ACID properties.
- The stored procedure or SQL submission automatically returns control to the parent transaction.

Update Propagation (UP)
UP is used for updating remote data with distributed atomicity and durability properties synchronized with the updates of the parent transaction. UPs may be implemented in the following way:

The parent transaction makes the UP "call" by storing a so-called *transaction record* in persistent storage at the parent location. The parent transaction id, the id of the subtransaction and the parameters of the subtransaction are stored in the transaction record. If the parent transaction fails, the transaction record will be rolled back and the subtransaction is not executed. If the parent transaction is committed, the transaction record is secured in persistent storage and we say that the UP has been *initiated.* After the initiation of the UP, the transaction record will be sent by the UP tool to the location of the corresponding subtransaction. The data transfer may be implemented by using push and/or pull technology. In contrast to RPCs, UPs have the following properties:

- If a parent transaction initiates several UPs, the corresponding, stored programs may be executed in parallel.
- A stored program initiated from a UP has atomicity synchronized with the parent transaction, i.e. either both or none of the transactions will be executed.
- The stored program does not automatically return control to the parent transaction.

In the following subsections, we will present a general outline of how relaxed ACID properties are implemented in the countermeasure transaction model.

2.1 The Atomicity Property

The *atomicity* property is normally implemented by a DBMS that ensures that either all or none of its updates of a transaction will be executed. In the countermeasure transaction model, the global transaction is partitioned into several local subtransactions with local ACID properties. Therefore, the global transaction does not have any of the global ACID properties. However, the global atomicity property can be implemented if the global transaction is divided into the following types of subtransactions:

1. The *pivot* subtransaction that manages the commitment of the global transaction. The global transaction is committed when the pivot subtransaction is committed locally. If the pivot subtransaction aborts, all the updates of the other subtransactions must be compensated.
2. The *compensatable* subtransactions that all may be compensated. Compensatable subtransactions must always be executed before the pivot subtransaction is executed to make it possible to compensate them if the pivot subtransaction cannot be committed. A compensatable subtransaction can be compensated by executing a compensating subtransaction.
3. The *retriable* subtransactions that are designed in such a way that the execution is guaranteed to commit locally (sooner or later) if the pivot subtransaction has been committed. A UP tool is used to resubmit the request for execution automatically until the subtransaction has been committed locally, i.e. the UP tool is used to force execution of the retriable subtransaction.

The global atomicity property is implemented by executing all the compensatable subtransactions and then the pivot subtransactions. If the pivot subtransaction fails, it is possible to compensate all the compensatable subtransactions, and therefore the atomicity property is secured. If the pivot subtransaction commits, all the retriable subtransactions will be initiated, and therefore the retriable subtransactions will be (r)executed automatically until they have been committed.

RPCs can be used to call/start the compensatable subtransactions and/or a pivot subtransaction as the execution of these subtransactions is not mandatory. It is always possible to initiate compensation if only the pivot is executed as the last subtransaction.

After the pivot subtransactions have committed, all the remaining updates are mandatory, and therefore the retriable subtransactions should always be initiated by UPs.

2.2 The Consistency Property

A database is *consistent* if its data complies with the consistency rules of the database. If the database is consistent both when a transaction starts and when it has been completed and committed, the execution has the *consistency property*.

Databases with relaxed ACID properties are almost always inconsistent, and therefore the consistency property cannot be fulfilled. However, in databases with relaxed ACID properties, *asymptotic consistency* is important:

If the database is asymptotically consistent when a transaction starts and also when it has been committed, the execution has the *relaxed consistency property*.

Without this property, it is impossible to implement consistent OLAP data warehouses on top of the inconsistent distributed OLTP database.

2.3 The Isolation Property

The *isolation property* ensures that the updates of a transaction are not seen by other transactions before the updates have been committed. Normally, the isolation property is implemented by the *concurrency control* [14] of the DBMS. In the countermeasure transaction model, the global transaction is partitioned into several local subtransactions with local ACID properties. Therefore, the global transaction does not have the global isolation property. If transactions are executed without isolation, the so-called *isolation anomalies* may occur. In the countermeasure transaction model, the consequences of these anomalies are prevented or reduced by using countermeasures. If there is no isolation, the following isolation anomalies may occur [15] and [16].

- *The lost update anomaly* is by definition a situation where a first transaction reads a record for update without using locks. Subsequently, the record is updated by another transaction. Later, the update is overwritten by the first transaction. The lost update anomaly may occur if a record is read and updated in different subtransactions as a second transaction may update the record between the read and the update of the first transaction. This may happen in the countermeasure transaction model, as records are not locked across a dialog with the user.
- *The dirty read anomaly* is by definition a situation where a first transaction updates a record without committing the update. Subsequently, a second transaction reads the record. Later, the first update is aborted (or committed), i.e. the second transaction may have read a non-existing version of the record. The dirty read anomaly may occur when a compensatable subtransaction updates a record and later aborts the update by using a compensating subtransaction. If another transaction reads the record before the update has been compensated, the data read will be "dirty".
- *The non-repeatable read anomaly* or *fuzzy read* is by definition a situation where a first transaction reads a record without using locks. Later, the record is updated and committed by a second transaction before the first transaction has been committed. Therefore, if the first transaction rereads the record, it may find that the data has changed. In extended transaction models, this may occur if a record is read and updated in different subtransactions as a second transaction may update the record between the read and the reread for the update. In the countermeasure transaction model, this may happen as records are not locked across a dialog with the user.
- *The phantom anomaly* is not relevant to this application area.

In the following, we will describe the countermeasures illustrated later in the example in section 4. We will first describe countermeasures against the lost update anomaly as these are most important.

The reread countermeasure can prevent the lost update anomaly that may occur if a global transaction reads a record in one subtransaction and later rereads the record for update in another transaction. If a second transaction has changed the record between the two reads, the transaction aborts itself after the second read to avoid overwriting the update of the second transaction. Often, it is not acceptable to lock records across a dialog with a user, and in this situation the reread countermeasure may be used to protect against the lost update anomaly. The reread countermeasure cannot be used in retriable subtransactions as these cannot be rejected.

The commutative updates countermeasure can prevent lost updates merely by using commutative operations like adding and subtracting an amount from an account. Subtransactions that only have commutative updates may be designed as commutable with other subtransactions that also only have commutative updates. The commutative updates countermeasure can prevent lost updates from retriable subtransactions. However, the commutative updates countermeasure can also prevent the lost updates that may occur if a second transaction updates a record between the updates of a compensatable subtransaction and its corresponding compensating subtransaction.

The pessimistic view countermeasure can reduce the consequences of a dirty read or a non-repeatable read by presenting the users with such a pessimistic view of the record that the users cannot misuse the information. The pessimistic view countermeasure may be implemented in the following way:

- Updates that reduce the users' options should be executed in the pivot or in the compensatable subtransactions. If these types of updates are aborted or compensated, it is impossible to misuse the reduced options.
- Updates that increase the users' options should be executed in the pivot or in the retriable subtransactions. As retriable subtransactions are executed after the global commit, it is impossible to misuse the increased options.

2.4 The Durability Property

Transactions have the *durability property* if the updates are stored in stable storage and secured by a log recovery system. The global durability property will automatically be implemented if the transactions have global atomicity and the local DBMS systems have local durability [16].

3 Description of the Most Important Replication Methods

In Table 1, the most important types of replication methods are evaluated together with the no-replication design as described by Frank [12]. Some of the properties are evaluated as Best, Average, Worst, Below average, etc., which allows us to compare the designs relatively. It has not been possible to select one of the replication designs as the best because the designs' properties vary according to the different evaluation criteria. Anyway, the table makes it possible to select the most inexpensive design

Table 1. Evaluation overview of replication designs

Properties	DBMS supported replication methods						
	n-safe design	Quorum-safe design	1-safe design. Basic solution	1-safe design with commutative updates	0-safe design with local commit	0-safe designs with deferred commit	No-replication design
Read performance/ capacity	Best	Worst	Average	Average	Best	Best	Average
Write performance	Worst	Above worst	Average	Average	Best	Below best	Average
Ease of failure recovery	Average	Average	Worst	Average	Best	Best	Average
Ease of disaster recovery	Best	Below best	Above worst	Average	Average	Average	Worst
The probability of lost data	Best. p^n	Below best $p^{\lceil n/2 \rceil}$	Worst p	Average	Average	Average	Worst p
Logging of the update transaction	Not supported	Not supported	Not supported	Recommended	Recommended	Recommended	Not supported
Availability	$1-q^n$	$1-q^n$	$1-q^n$	$1-q^n$	$1-q^n$	$1-q^n$	$1-q$
Atomicity	Best	Best	Worst	Best	Best	Best	Best
Consistency	Best	Best	Average	Average	Worst	Worst	Best
Isolation	Best	Best	Average	Average	Worst	Worst	Best
Durability	Best	Best	Worst	Best	Best	Best	Best

that fulfills the needs of a specific application. In the following, we will give a short description of the evaluation criteria used in table 1. In Frank [12], you will find a more detailed description of the evaluation.

The read performance/capacity of a table design is evaluated to be the "best" if remote readings always can be substituted by local readings. The read performance/capacity is evaluated as worse, the more remote reads the replication design needs.

The write performance/capacity of a table design is evaluated to be the "best" if a global table update always can be committed locally without communication with other locations. The write performance/capacity is evaluated as worse, the more remote accesses the replication design needs before a write/update can be committed.

After local *failure*, the local database and its log files are not physically destroyed, and therefore it is always possible to repair the site. The *ease with which failure recovery can be achieved* is evaluated as "best" if the system automatically can make recovery without aborting all non-committed transactions in case of site failure. The ease with which failure recovery can be achieved is evaluated as worse, the more recovery work it takes to abort or commit non-committed transactions in case of site failure.

A database disaster is as a situation where a local database and its log files are destroyed. *The ease with which disaster recovery can be achieved* is evaluated as "best" if it is possible to repair the database automatically. The ease with which disaster recovery can be achieved is evaluated as worse, the more recovery work it takes to abort or commit non-committed transactions in case of site disaster. Full recovery after a disaster may be impossible if only an old remote database copy can be used for recovery.

The probability of lost data is mathematically defined as a value between 0 and 1, and the probability can often be calculated as a function of the probability, say p, of a local disaster and the number n of sites that may fail. The probability of lost data is better the closer the value is to 0.

It is assumed that *logging of the update transactions in the locations of the clients* is necessary for some replication designs to avoid losing transactions in case of disaster. If this property is recommended, it is assumed that it is implemented where the evaluation criteria *ease with which disaster recovery can be done* and *availability* are evaluated.

The *availability* of a database is defined as the probability of having access to the database. The availability is a function of the probability, say q, of local site failure, which depends on the probability of disasters, failures and the time it takes to repair the situations.

The ACID properties have been defined earlier in this paper, and they are evaluated to be "best" if they are supported by a DBMS product. The ACID properties are evaluated as worse, the more manual work it requires to implement or compensate for the missing properties.

The development costs of a table design are evaluated to be "best" if there is no need for special application programming, i.e. all replication problems are managed by using DBMS tools. The development costs are evaluated as worse, the more manual work it takes to develop and implement the replication design.

3.1   The n-Safe Design with the ROWA Protocol and the 2-Safe Design

In the n-safe design [14], the coordinating transaction manager commits a global update if and only if all other n-1 participating transaction managers commit the update locally. There are many versions of the n-safe design. In all the versions, it is possible to optimize the write performance by not forcing the log records to durable storage before they are sent. This is acceptable in the n-safe design because in case of a disaster, it is extremely unlikely that all n copies of the log are involved in the disaster. The 2-safe design is a special case of the n-safe design where only two copies of a file exist.

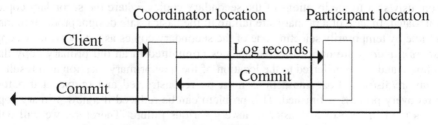

Fig. 1. 2-safe database design

In the ROWA (Read One Write All) protocol, only one lock is needed to read a record while all copies must be locked before an update can take place. Therefore, the n-safe design with the ROWA protocol has the best read performance while the write performance is evaluated as worst.

The ROWA protocol is very vulnerable to both communication and site failures. The ROWAA (Read One, Write All Available) protocol is a new version of the ROWA protocol. It is tolerant to both communication and site failures at the costs of controlling that all participating copies are available when the transaction is committed. However, this extra control reduces the performance for all transactions. In stable networks where failures are rare, it is therefore much better to restart the traditional ROWA protocol with a new value of n in case of communication or site failures.

3.2   The n-Safe Design with the Quorum Protocol

The *quorum consensus protocol* is tolerant to both communication and site failures as only a number of locations with a 'quorum' is necessary to access the data. In the quorum consensus protocol, a number of 'votes' is assigned to each copy. Each read operation must obtain a read quorum R before it can execute the read operation, and each write/update operation must obtain a write quorum W before it can execute the write/update. In order to obtain the isolation property, R and W must be selected in such a way that W is greater than half the amount of votes and R+W are greater than the total number of votes. If R = 1, W = the number of locations with a copy, and each location has one vote, the quorum consensus protocol specializes itself to the ROWA protocol, and therefore it is assumed in the following that R is greater than 2. In this case, the ROWA protocol has a better read performance than the quorum consensus protocol as the ROWA protocol only has to read one copy. The quorum consensus protocol has a better write performance than the ROWA protocol as the quorum consensus protocol only has to lock W copies before it is possible to write/update replicated data. The quorum consensus protocol provides better availability than the ROWA protocol as the quorum consensus protocol can tolerate some communication and site failures.

3.3   The Basic 1-Safe Design

The basic 1-safe design [14] has a primary copy of the data that first must be updated under normal operation. An update is committed when the primary copy update is committed locally. After the primary copy has been committed, the log record is asynchronously sent to the locations of the secondary copies, where the secondary copies are updated. In case of a primary site failure in the basic1-safe design, production may continue by temporarily selecting one of the secondary copies as a new primary copy. *Lost transactions* are defined as the updates committed in an old primary copy that has failed and not transferred to the location of the new primary location as a result of the failure/disaster. Lost transactions must be reconstructed and re-executed before the recovery process is finished. This problem can be reduced if a new primary copy only is used in case of a disaster or a very serious failure. Therefore, we will only recommend the basic 1-safe design in ERP tables when the updates can be executed well in advance before they are needed. In this way, it is possible to use the cheap basic 1-safe design with a very low risk of lost transactions.

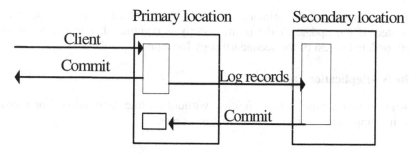

Fig. 2. 1-safe database design

3.4 The 0-Safe Design with Local Commit

In *the 0-safe design with local commit,* an update transaction will go to the nearest database location, where it is executed and committed both globally and locally. Next, retriable subtransactions are propagated asynchronously to the other database locations, where they are re-executed without user dialog and committed locally at each location. As retriable updates may be initiated from any location, the different table copies will often be inconsistent. As described earlier, the commutative updates countermeasure may prevent retriable transactions from making lost updates.

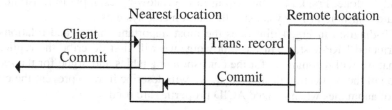

Fig. 3. 0-safe database design

3.5 The 1-Safe Design with Commutative Updates

In *the 1-safe design with commutative updates,* the updates are transferred to the secondary copies in the same way as the 0-safe design with local commit, i.e. after the global commit in the primary copy location, retriable subtransactions are initiated for updating the secondary copies. In this design, lost transactions cannot occur because the retriable subtransactions will be executed sooner or later. The lost update anomaly can be prevented in the same way as described under the 0-safe design with local commit.

3.6 The 0-Safe Designs with Deferred Commit

In the *"0-safe designs with deferred commit",* an update transaction will go to the nearest database location where it is executed and committed locally, but not globally. Later, the update may be committed globally in a variety of ways depending on the different versions of the replication method. In *the 0-safe design with primary copy commit,* the global transaction is committed/rejected in a (remote) primary copy location. If the update of the primary copy is rejected, the first local update must be compensated. If the update of the primary copy is committed, retriable subtransactions will update the rest of the secondary copy locations.

3.7 The No-Replication Design

The no-replication design is by definition without on-line replication. For recovery reasons, it is important to store remote off-line copies.

4   Implementation of Relaxed ACID Properties in Distributed ERP Software

In a distributed ERP system, each local ERP system can use the resources/stocks managed by the other local ERP systems. Many major companies have a physically distributed sales and/or production organization. In such organizations, a distributed ERP system may be useful. In this section, we will integrate the nested transaction model described in section 2 with the different replication designs described in section 3 to design a distributed ERP system with high performance and availability. By using table 1's evaluation overview, it is possible to select the most inexpensive table design that fulfills the needs of an application. The following example illustrates how this might be done. Frank [13] has also used the following example to illustrate how to integrate distributed ERP systems with E-commerce systems.

The ER-diagram in Fig. 4 illustrates the most important entities and relationships in a distributed ERP system. In the following, we will first describe the replication design that we will recommend for the corresponding tables and argue for the recommendation of the replication design. Next, we will describe how to prevent the consequences of anomalies when relaxed ACID properties are used.

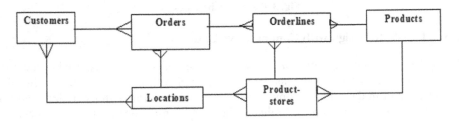

Fig. 4. ER Diagram of an example distributed ERP system

The Location table is needed in all locations as it is used in the Orderlines to indicate which store should deliver the products. We will recommend that the Location table uses the basic 1-safe design with a central primary copy. The reason why we recommend this design is that it is the cheapest replication design, and as the organization will know well in advance when new locations are created it should be possible to create secondary copies long time before they are needed. Therefore, if a failure occurs in the primary copy location, it is possible to defer all updates until the failure has been repaired, i.e. no lost transactions will occur. In other words, no risks are taken by using the inexpensive basic 1-safe design.

We will also recommend that the Product table uses the basic 1-s4. Implementation of Relaxed ACID Properties in Distributed ERP Software safe design with a central primary copy and secondary copies in all the remote locations. The reason why we recommend this design is that the organization should know well in advance when new products are created or changed. However, hard local competition may force the organization to effectuate a quick local price change. In this situation, local prices should be stored in a local table. The local Price tables do not need replication if the prices of the selling location are used. This is the fairest solution as the buyer need not know that the local branch office is out of stock.

We will recommend that the customer table for local customers is fragmented and uses the basic 1-safe design with the primary copies in the locations that deal with the local customers. The secondary copies should be stored in the central location where they are used for backup, data warehousing, and control of whether a new customer is local or not.

We will recommend that the customer table for customers who deal with more than one branch office is fragmented and uses the 1-safe design with the primary copy in the central location. The secondary copies should be stored in all the locations where the customer has placed orders previously. The balance of a customer must be updated each time an Order is invoiced. First, the balance should be updated in the local Customer record. Later, the updating should be committed globally at the central primary copy. From here, the other remote branch offices involved will (sooner or later) receive the updates committed in the central primary copy location.

However, in practice it may be necessary for a common Customer table to use the 0-safe design with local commit because often a basic 1-safe design tool cannot tolerate primary copies in different locations.

We will recommend that the Order table uses the 1-safe design. Normally, Orders are only used in the locations where the sales took place. Therefore, we will recommend that the Order table is fragmented with the primary copy stored in the location of the seller. A secondary copy should be stored in the central location for backup and data warehousing purposes.

We will recommend that the Product-stock table is fragmented in such a way that each store location has its own Product-stock records. Each fragment of the Product-stock table should have the no-replication design, as it is too expensive to replicate a stock record for each update. (A snapshot copy of the local Product-stock fragments should be stored for backup in the central location).

We will recommend that the Orderline table is fragmented and uses the 0-safe design with primary copy commit in the location where the stock is reduced to fulfill the order line. A secondary copy should be stored in the location that created the order. However, the Orderline should always first be created in the database of the order location. Later, the Orderline will be committed globally in a stock location where a primary copy will be created.

When a salesman makes a new order, the salesman must first access or create a customer record in the sales location. Next, a compensatable subtransaction will create an order record with relationship to the customer record. The salesman can now make order-lines. For each new order-line, a compensatable subtransaction will create an order-line and start a compensatable sub-subtransaction that updates the stock level of the product ordered in the order-line (the pessimistic view countermeasure is used). If the local stock location cannot fulfill the quantity ordered in the order-line, a compensatable sub-subtransaction will be initiated for execution in another stock location, etc. If an order-line cannot be fulfilled, a compensatable subtransaction must update the field 'quantity-delivered' in the order-line. The pivot subtransaction that updates the account of the customer will be executed when all the order-lines have been confirmed by the servers of the stores. The pivot subtransaction has retriable subtransactions that update replicated customers.

In a distributed ERP system, the E-commerce system is integrated as any other location, and therefore the E-commerce system can operate with or without its own stocks as any other location [15].

5 Related Work

Different versions of the 1-safe and 2-safe designs have been described in e.g. [2], [3], [4] and [5]. The "0-safe design with local commit" has been described by Frank and Zahle [1] and used in practice for a number of years . The 2-safe designs, the basic 1-safe design, "the 1-safe design with commutative updates" and "the 0-safe design with local commit" have all been described and evaluated in detail by Frank [6]. The transaction model described in section 2 is *the countermeasure transaction model* described in [1] and [7]. This model owes many of its properties to e.g. Garcia-Molina and Salem [8]; Mehrotra et al. [9]; Weikum and Schek [10] and Zhang [11].

The evaluation of replication designs used in this paper have been described by Frank [12]. Many new versions of the classic replication designs have been described in recent years. The most important versions have been described on the basis of the corresponding classic design. All the classic replication designs may be optimized by group communication. However, group communication does not change the relative evaluation of the replication designs if group communication is used in all the designs that are compared.

An architecture for integrating a distributed ERP system with an E-commerce system has been described by Frank [13].

6 Conclusions and Future Research

In a distributed ERP system, the different local ERP systems are integrated in such a way that each local system can use the resources/stocks managed by the other local ERP systems. In this paper, we have described how it is possible to integrate local autonomous ERP systems in such a way that they function as a distributed ERP system. In addition, the techniques used for integrating the systems can improve performance and availability.

The reason we call our model *distributed ERP system architecture* is because we use a general transaction model with relaxed ACID properties that can support many different replication designs related to the common conceptual ERP database. In the same way, it is possible to make distributed architectures for other enterprise application areas to optimize performance, availability, and integration with other systems.

However, not all types of systems can be integrated as easily as ERP systems. The reason is that special replication anomalies may occur when 1-safe and 0-safe designs are used. These anomalies are not important in distributed ERP systems. However, we have started a project aiming to describe where replication anomalies are important and how to deal with them. Hopefully, Frank [17] will soon be able to publish the first results of this project.

References

1. Frank, L. and Zahle, T, 1998, "Semantic ACID Properties in Multidatabases Using Remote Procedure Calls and Update Propagations", Software - Practice & Experience, Vol.28, pp77-98.
2. Garcia-Molina, H. and Polyzois, C., 1990, "Issues in disaster recovery", IEEE Compcon., IEEE, New York, pp 573-577.
3. Polyzois, C. and Garcia-Molina, H., 1994, "Evaluation of Remote Backup Algorithms for Transaction-Processing Systems", ACM TODS, 19(3), pp 423-449.
4. Gallersdörfer, R. and Nicola, M., 1995, "Improving Performance in Replicated Databases through Relaxed Coherency", Proc 21st VLDB Conf, 1995, pp 445-455.
5. Humborstad, R., Sabaratnam, M., Hvasshovd, S. and Torbjornsen, O., 1997, "1-Safe algorithms for symmetric site configurations", Proc 23th VLDB Conf, 1997, pp 316-325.
6. Frank, L., 1999, 'Evaluation of the Basic Remote Backup and Replication Methods for High Availability Databases', Software - Practice & Experience, Vol. 29, issue 15, pp 1339-1353.
7. Frank, L and Kofod, U, 2002, 'Atomicity Implementation in E-Commerce Systems', Proc of the Second International Conference on Electronic Commerce, ICEB 2002, Taipei, pp381-383.
8. Garcia-Molina, H. and Salem, K., 1987, "Sagas", ACM SIGMOD Conf, pp 249-259.
9. Mehrotra, S., Rastogi, R., Korth, H., and Silberschatz, A., 1992, "A transaction model for multi-database systems", Proc International Conference on Distributed Computing Systems, pp 56-63.
10. Weikum, G. and Schek, H., 1992, "Concepts and Applications of Multilevel Transactions and Open Nested Transactions", A. Elmagarmid (ed.): Database Transaction Models for Advanced Applications, Morgan Kaufmann, pp 515-553.
11. Zhang, A., Nodine, M., Bhargava, B. and Bukhres, O., 1994, "Ensuring Relaxed Atomicity for Flexible Transactions in Multidatabase Systems", Proc ACM SIGMOD Conf, pp 67-78.
12. Frank, L., 2005, "Replication Methods and Their Properties", published in: Laura C. Rivero, Jorge H. Doorn, Viviana E. Ferraggine (Editors), Encyclopedia of Database Technologies and Applications, Idea Group Inc..
13. Frank, L., 2004, 'Architecture for Integration of Distributed ERP Systems and E-commerce Systems', Industrial Management and Data Systems (IMDS), Vol. 104(5), pp 418-429.
14. Gray, J. and Reuter, A., 1993, "Transaction Processing", Morgan Kaufman, 1993.
15. Berenson, H., Bernstein, P., Gray, J., Melton, J., O'Neil, E. and O'Neil, P., 1995, "A Critique of ANSI SQL Isolation Levels", Proc ACM SIGMOD Conf., pp. 1-10.
16. Breibart, Y., Garcia-Molina, H. and Silberschatz, A., 1992, "Overview of Multidatabase Transaction Management", VLDB Journal, 2, pp 181-239.
17. Frank, L. 2006, 'Databases with Relaxed ACID Properties', a doctoral thesis submitted for the Dr. Merc. degree, Copenhagen Business School. The thesis will probably be accepted and published in 2006.

Influence of Balancing Used in a Distributed Data Warehouse on the Extraction Process

Marcin Gorawski and Pawel Marks

Silesian University of Technology, Institute of Computer Science,
Akademicka 16 street, 44-101 Gliwice, Poland
{Marcin.Gorawski, Pawel.Marks}@polsl.pl

Abstract. A data warehouse is filled with data during the extraction process. Such a process is sometimes interrupted by occurrence of a failure. After a failure the warehouse contains an incomplete data set, a part of the set is missing. To load the missing part of the data one of the interrupted extraction resumption algorithms is usually used. In this paper we analyze the influence of data balancing used in a distributed data warehouse on the efficiency of extraction and resumption processes. During resumption we base on the Design-Resume algorithm which imposes no additional overhead on an uninterrupted extraction process. We present how the balancing is done and examine its influence on the ETL process efficiency. Finally, basing on the results of performed tests, we discuss advantages and disadvantages of the balancing with respect to the ETL process.

1 Introduction

During the ETL process (*Extraction Transformation and Loading*) large amounts of data are transformed and loaded to a data warehouse. It takes a very long time, several hours or even days. There is usually a relatively small time window fixed for a whole extraction. The more data to be processed, the longer the ETL process. Interruption of the process, for example due to hardware failure or lack of power supply, leaves the data warehouse with an incomplete data set, which renders the warehouse unusable. To fix the situation the extraction must be restarted. Such a situation is not rare. In a Sagent Technologies report it is said that statistically every thirty extraction process is interrupted by a failure [7]. After an interruption there is usually no time left for rerunning the extraction from the beginning. In this case, the most efficient solution is to apply one of the interrupted extraction resumption algorithms. In this paper we analyze the standard Design-Resume [5] algorithm (DR) featuring our modifications, and a combination of DR and staging technique (hybrid resumption). The modified DR handles extraction graphs containing many extractors and many inserters.

Most commercial tools or tools like Ajax [2] do not consider the internal structure of transformations and the graph architecture of ETL processes. Exceptions are researches [8,9], where the authors describe the ETL ARKTOS

D. Draheim and G. Weber (Eds.): TEAA 2005, LNCS 3888, pp. 84–98, 2006.

(ARKTOS II) tool. To optimize the ETL process, there is often designed a dedicated extraction application adjusted to requirements of a particular data warehouse system. Our experience prompted the decision to build a developmental ETL environment using JavaBeans components. In the meantime, a similar approach was proposed in [1].

Further speeding up of the ETL process forced us to abandon the JavaBeans platform. The ETL-DR environment succeeds the previous ETL/JB (JavaBeans ETL environment) and DR/JB (ETL environment with DR resumption support). The new ETL-DR environment is a set of Java object classes, used to build extraction and resumption applications. This is analogous to JavaBeans components in the DR/JB environment. In the DR/JB we implemented an estimation mechanism detecting cases when the use of DR resumption is inefficient. Unfortunately, the model we used did not take into account many significant external factors, like virtual memory usage. In the ETL-DR the situation changed. We improved the implementation of the DR filters, which resulted in reduction of resumption inefficiency. Now the resumption is almost always faster than restarting the extraction from the beginning. Hence, we decided to stop research on this mechanism. Another direction of our research is combining the DR resumption with techniques like staging and checkpointing. Similar research was presented in [5] where the authors compared the DR algorithm to its combination with savepoints. They proved that the DR-savepoint combination performs a little better than the pure DR. Unfortunately these experiments were performed on very small TCP-D data sets . In our opinion opinion it gives non-representative results, because in datawarehousing we have to deal with much larger datasets than presented in [5]. In our implementation of the staging technique the data transferred between nodes are also saved on a disk. After a failure the data can be restored from the disk and there is no need process it again. Its disadvantages are the quite big overhead imposed on the extraction processes by data saves and, in some cases, loss of processing parallelism. In checkpointing, the state of the whole extraction process is periodically saved. After a failure the processing is reverted to the latest checkpoint. Unfortunately, the implementation of checkpointing is not easy and often requires a lot of transformations modification. We gave the name "hybrid resumption" to the combination of DR and staging. This approach performs better than pure DR algorithm. Research on checkpointing is in progress.

In distributed systems it is important to utilize the computing power optimally. This prompts system designers to use various balancing algorithms. In our data warehouse the problem of balancing is also important. The more the performance of machines comprising the warehouse differs, the more complicated the balancing. We decided to use the partitioning algorithm for fact tables only. All the other dimension tables are replicated on the machines without any modification [4]. Such a balancing algorithm worked well and satisfied our expectations. We now seek to analyze its influence on the efficiency of the extraction process.

Section 2 briefly describes the basic and modified DR algorithms. The hybrid resumption algorithm is described in Sect. 3. In Sect. 4 is our test environment, and in Sect. 5 the general balancing algorithm is described. Resumption tests with results and short comments are in Sect. 6. In Sect. 7 the obtained results are discussed and the paper is summarized.

2   Design-Resume Algorithm

2.1   Basic Version of the Algorithm

The Design-Resume[5, 6] algorithm (DR) works using properties assigned to each node of the extraction graph and data already loaded to a destination prior to a failure. This algorithm belongs to the group of redo algorithms, but during resumption it uses additional filters that remove from the data stream all tuples contributing to the tuples already loaded (Fig. 1). An extraction graph is a directed acyclic graph (DAG), whose nodes process data and whose edges define data flow directions.

The algorithm is divided into two phases. In phase 1 the extraction graph is analyzed and additional filters are assigned (Design procedure). In phase 2 the filters are initialized with data already loaded into a data warehouse (Resume procedure). The most important feature of the DR algorithm is that it does not impose any additional overhead on the uninterrupted extraction process. Algorithms like staging or savepointing usually increase processing time a lot (as many as several times). The drawback of the DR algorithm is that it cannot be applied if before a failure no output data were produced. Design procedure is usually run once to assign filters that are needed during resumption. The Resume procedure is run each time the ETL process must be resumed. It fetches data already loaded from a destination, and uses the data to initialize additional filters assigned in phase 1.

The basic DR algorithm, denoted later as DR(1), can resume efficiently only a single-inserter extraction graph (an inserter is a loading node). This limitation lowers the resumption efficiency, and encouraged us to modify the algorithm.

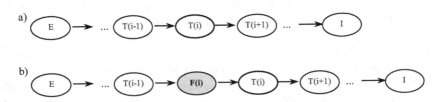

Fig. 1. Examples of simple extraction (a) and a resumption (b) graphs. E is an extractor node reading data from a source. T stands for a transformation node, such as filtration, grouping etc. I is an inserter loading data to a destination (a database table, for instance). Graph (b) also contains additional filter node F. This node removes from a data stream all tuples contributing only to the tuples already loaded to the destination. Such a filter can be inserted on each edge of the extraction graph. Before running the resumption it is initialized using data already loaded by the inserter.

2.2   The Algorithm Modifications

The DR algorithm's limitation disallowing the resumption of ETL processes with many loading nodes is quite burdensome. The extraction graph must be divided into segments containing one inserter each. Usually the data loaded by one of the inserters are transformed by the same set of transformations as the data loaded by another inserter. It is 100% true for distributed warehouses where some of the tables are duplicated on the machines comprising the warehouse. Dividing the graph into smaller parts and running them independently forces some transformations to be run twice or more to do the same job. This time waste would be eliminated if the original extraction graph was used for resumption. To improve the algorithm we modified both Design and Resume procedures.

The first modification was analysis of which inserters are necessary during resumption, and which have already completed the loading process. It is possible because each inserter, after loading, writes its ID into the list of inserters that finished the processing. The list is kept in an external disk file. Before resumption the list is loaded from the file, and all inserters found on the list are removed from the extraction graph. After removing the inserters, the transformations that lost their destination nodes are removed also. In this manner we obtain the resumption graph limited to the inserters that must be resumed and the transformations and extractors processing data for them. This modification has the biggest impact on the overall resumption efficiency. It also forces the DR filters assignation routine to be run before each resumption, because the graph structure changes.

Next, we introduced a transitive property sameSuffix. It was mentioned by the DR algorithm authors in [5] but it was not developed. This property let us to assign DR filters more optimally, and closer to extractors. Its influence is mostly visible when the processing path divides into many paths performing similar operations but loading data by separate inserters. Such a situation occurs in distributed data warehouses.

After defining a new property we changed filter assignation rules. Now data stream can be filtered in a common part of the graph even if it is targeted to many inserters. We also had to modify the definition of the redundant filter, and change the DR filters' structure [5].

3   Hybrid Resumption

The general idea of the hybrid resumption is quite simple. It is a combined resumption algorithm taking advantage of both the Design-Resume algorithm and the staging technique. A similar approach combining the DR and savepoints was examined in [5]. During a normal extraction process, each node previously selected by the graph designer generates output data, sends it to the consecutive nodes, and also writes each output tuple to a temporary disk file. When the node finishes processing, the file it generates is marked as containing a complete data set. The difference between savepoints and staging is, in staging technique there are no periodical writes to external files. Only output tuples are stored in a file,

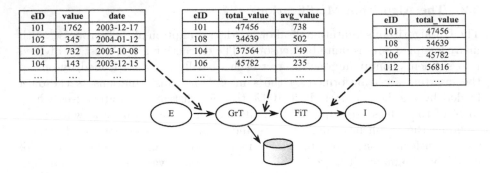

Fig. 2. Example of ETL process with staging technique

not the state of a whole node, as in savepoints. An example of an extraction graph to which staging is applied presents Fig. 2. Node E is an extractor, that reads data from a source (database or file). The grouping node GrT works in staging mode; it writes transitional (already produced) data to a disk file denoted by "⌷". The filter node FiT performs a simple filtration, and all the result tuples are stored in a destination by inserter (loading node) I.

Extraction may be interrupted by a failure before or after the entire transitional data file (or files) is written. When failure occurs without completing the file, only a standard DR resumption can be applied. But, if the file is marked as containing a complete data set, hybrid resumption can be used. In the first step, from the extraction graph are removed all the nodes that correspond only to the nodes working in staging mode. These nodes are unnecessary because they do not need to be run again to get already-written transitional data. As can be seen in Fig. 3, nodes E and GrT are removed. Next, the transitional data file is connected as a source for FiT node. The modified graph is then analyzed with the DR algorithm. As a result of the analysis an additional filter F_{CP}, is inserted

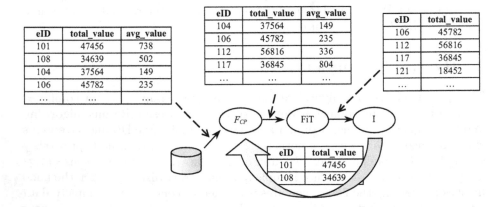

Fig. 3. Hybrid resumption after occurrence of a failure

before the node FiT (Fig. 3). The filter is initialized with a part of the tuple set loaded prior to a failure. Now the normal extraction process using the modified extraction graph is started. Summing up, the staging part reduces the number of nodes that have to be run during resumption, and the DR part reduces the amount of data that must be processed.

Currently, we do not try to use incomplete transitional data files. Our goal is to increase the resumption performance without imposing overhead on the normal extraction process (not interrupted). To achieve it, we select for writing transitional data files only the nodes that significantly reduce tuple stream size, for instance aggregation or highly selective filtration. Aggregation nodes consume tuples from input streams, and when the stream ends, they start producing an output set. In most cases the time of producing an output set is much shorter than the time spent on receiving and processing an input set. The possibility is very low that a failure occurs between opening and closing a transitional data file. When we deal with the filtration the situation is different. In such case, output tuples are produced on the fly; each accepted tuple is automatically stored in the file. Use of such a file is possible even if it is incomplete.

3.1 Hybrid Resumption in Theory

Given a graph path started with an extractor E, ended by an inserter I and containing an ordered sequence of transformations $T(i)$ (see Fig. 4), let us analyze what actions must be taken in order to properly restart an extraction process interrupted by a failure.

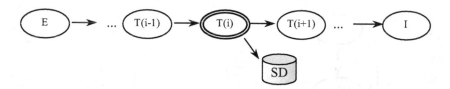

Fig. 4. Graph path with one node using staging mode

An extractor produces tuples; they are transformed in nodes $T(1) - T(i-1)$. In node $T(i)$ the tuples not only are processed and sent to the subsequent node, they are also immediately stored in a stage data file SD without any unnecessary delay. The moment of failure cannot be predicted; we assume it may happen at any time. Three cases can be distinguished:

- no tuples are stored in SD file (or the file does not even exist),
- SD file contains a part of the expected data set; node $T(i)$ is still running,
- SD file contains all tuples produced by node $T(i)$; the node is stopped.

If no SD data is available before restarting the interrupted ETL process, it means that the node $T(i)$ has not yet produced any tuples. In consequence it cannot be any tuple written to a destination by an inserter node. If there is no stage data and no tuples in the destination, then the only possible action to

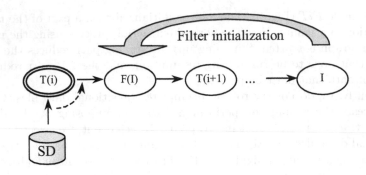

Fig. 5. Hybrid resumption when an SD file is complete

be taken is restarting the extraction, just like during the normal processing. No modification in a graph path is made.

The resumption is most efficient when the stage data file is complete. The complete data set must be recovered from the SD file and directly or indirectly sent to the input of node $T(i+1)$. If the inserter managed to load some data into a destination prior to a failure, then contributors of the loaded tuples do not need to reprocessed once again. These contributors should be removed from a tuple stream as soon as possible using DR algorithm filters. Such filters can be placed just behind the node recovering staging data (or somewhere else between $T(i)$ and I) and it needs to be initialized with data taken from the inserter I (Fig. 5).

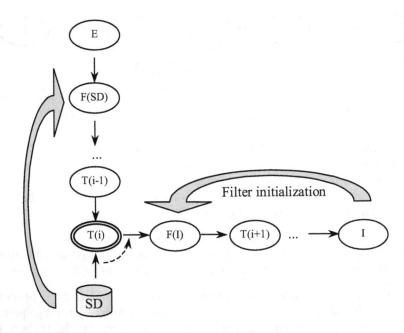

Fig. 6. Hybrid resumption when an SD file exists but it is incomplete

It can be any of the DR filter types, depending on the DR input properties set by the designer.

The most complicated case is when the stage data file contains some data, but it is not complete. To handle such a case efficiently, additional filtration must be performed before and behind the node $T(i)$ (Fig. 6). Filtration behind $T(i)$ is done in the same way as in the above case, when SD file is complete. To perform the filtration before node $T(i)$ one more filters must be inserted into the graph; depending on the DR properties of the nodes preceding $T(i)$ it can be of prefix or subset type. The closer to the extractor the filter is placed, the more efficient the resumption runs. The filter in comparison to a filter $F(I)$ in Fig. 5, is not initialized with data from the inserter, but its initialization set is taken from the SD file of the node $T(i)$.

Currently our hybrid resumption algorithm handles the cases when the stage data file (or files) does not exist or contains a complete tuple set. We have not implemented the incomplete SD file case yet, because in our research the simpler version's efficiency is sufficient. The extraction processes we run do not let us observe the benefits that the complete hybrid algorithm (with incomplete SD file handling) could offer. In our extraction graphs we do not have highly selective transformations performing on-the-fly processing (see Sect. 6).

4   ETL-DR Extraction Environment

The ETL-DR environment is written in Java; it is a successor to the DR/JB environment (see Sect. 1). However, in the new environment we do not use JavaBeans technology. We gambled on simplicity, efficiency, and ease of further development. The ETL-DR is a set of classes used by the graph designer to create an extraction application. These are analogous to JavaBeans components in the DR/JB environment. In comparison to the DR/JB, we significantly improved the processing efficiency and the complexity of the most important transformations, namely DR filters, grouping and joining.

Besides increasing the processing efficiency of the ETL-DR environment, the most important fact is that we implemented a modified DR algorithm within it (see Sect. 2.2). It enables the resumption of interrupted extraction processes described by graphs containing many loading nodes. Moreover, to take advantage of all the DR algorithm features, we use a modified algorithm of loading data into a database. Tuples are loaded in a way making the inserter suffix-safe [5], which means that the last loaded tuple is known. This can speed up the resumption process significantly.

5   Balancing Algorithm

Let us introduce the concept of a fact table division factor denoted by p_i [4]. Its value is a part of the fact table stored in the i node of the distributed warehouse system. Basing on the aggregation time, the p_i factor for each machine is iteratively computed. The goal of the balancing is to obtain node work time similar to the mean work time. The balancing algorithm is as follows:

1. Load dimension tables into all nodes in the same form.
2. Set all fact table division factors to $p_i = 1/N$, where N is the number of machines comprising the warehouse.
3. Load a test subset of fact table, partitioned according to the division factors into all nodes.
4. Perform test aggregation of the loaded set.
5. Compute imbalance factors. If maximum imbalance is smaller than assumed value, go to 7; otherwise go to 6.
6. Correct division factors p_i using the aggregation time values, go to 3.
7. Load a whole fact table, partitioned according to the last computed division factors into all nodes.

In the first step, dimension tables are loaded. The same data set is loaded into each node. The initial values of p_i factors are set to $1/N$ where N is the number of nodes. The next step of the algorithm is calculation of a fact table partition plan:

1. Calculate H/Z-value for the localization of each meter (see Sect. 6), where H denotes Hilbert curve and Z denotes Peano curve.
2. Sort meters according to H/Z-values in ascending order.
3. Allocate chunks to nodes using the round-robin method.

After loading the test data set, the test aggregation is performed and aggregation times are collected. In the next step the imbalance factors are computed in reference to the shortest time measured. If the maximum imbalance exceeds the assumed limit, the corrections are made to division factors and the process repeats. When the imbalance is small enough, then a final loading of a complete data set is run.

6   Tests

6.1   Test Conditions

The base for our tests is an extraction graph containing 4 extractors and 15 inserters (loading nodes). The graph consists of three independent parts, but it is seen by the extraction application as a single ETL process. To load data into a distributed data warehouse consisting of 5 PC machines we had to increase the number of inserters in the graph. Each inserter loads data into a single database table. Finally we obtained the graph containing 75 inserters.

The ETL process generates a complete data warehouse structure (Fig. 7). It is a distributed spatial data warehouse system designed for storing and analyzing a wide range of spatial data [3]. The data is generated by media meters working in a radio-based measurement system. All the data is gathered in a telemetric server, from which it can be fetched to fill the data warehouse. The distributed

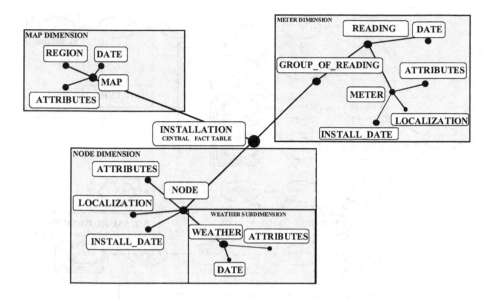

Fig. 7. Schema of the generated data warehouse

system is based on a new model called the cascaded star model. The test input data set size is 500MB.

The data set is distributed over the 5 PC machines. All the dimension tables are replicated and each machine gathers the same data set. The fact table containing measurements from remote meters is divided into 5 parts according to the result of the balancing algorithm described in Sect. 5. The inserters loading data into fact tables are preceded by additional filter nodes (see Fig. 8). Their task is to filter the tuples according to the distribution criteria. More detailed graph description can be found in Sect. 6.2.

The tests were divided into two parts. First the balancing process were run and the parameters for distribution filters were obtained. Then we ran a complete extraction process, loading both dimension and fact tables. The fact tables were distributed among the machines according to the balancing results.

During each loading test the extraction process was interrupted in order to simulate a failure. The resumption process was then run and the time was measured. The collected measurement results permitted us to prepare resumption charts showing the resumption efficiency depending on the time of a failure.

For the tests we used the following machines:

1. for ETL software:
   - 1x PIV 2.8GHz 512MB RAM, Windows XP Prof, J2SDK 1.4.2_06
2. for distributed data warehouse based on Oracle 9i database:
   - 1x PIV 2.8GHz 512MB RAM, Windows XP Prof
   - 2x PIV 2.8GHz 512MB RAM, Windows 2000
   - 2x PIV HT 3.2GHz 1GB RAM, Windows XP Prof

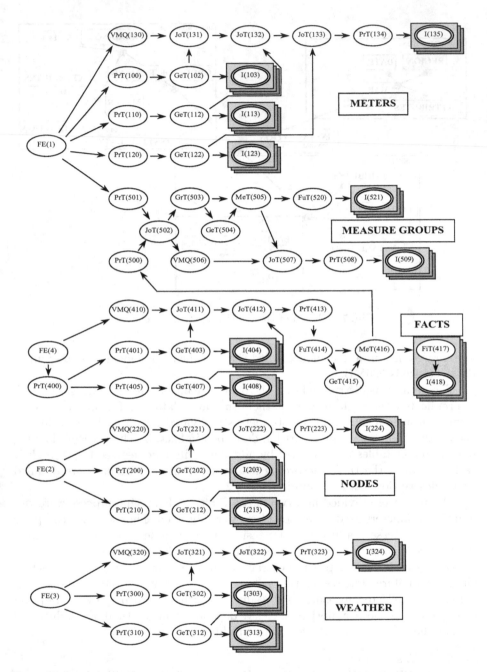

Fig. 8. Extraction graph used in distributed resumption tests. Inserters are marked with double line ovals. Each node enclosed in the shaded rectangle is duplicated as many times as there are destination machines comprising the warehouse. In our tests we used 5 PC machines. Node $FiT(417)$ is an additional filter used in fact table distribution process.

Communication with the database was implemented using JDBC interface and Oracle OCI drivers. Oracle SQL*Loader was also used for fast data loading into database tables. Portions of data were loaded into temporary tables by SQL*Loader, and simple INSERT queries moved the packets into target tables. A single uninterrupted extraction process lasts about 65 minutes.

6.2   Detailed Description of the Extraction Graph

Basing on Fig. 8, extractors read the following data from source files:

- $FE(1)$ - meters parameters (meterID, nodeID, locX, locY, locZ, type, scope, monDate),
- $FE(2)$ - weather changes around collecting nodes (nodeID, temperature, humidity, clouds, measDate),
- $FE(3)$ - collecting nodes parameters (nodeID, locX, locY, locZ, monDate),
- $FE(4)$ - set of meter measurements records (meterID, date, time, zone1, zone2).

Basing of the four source files, a complete data warehouse containing 15 tables is generated. METERS, NODES and WEATHER dimensions consists of the main table containing records describing particular meters, nodes or weather states, and also additional sub-dimension tables with necessary attributes. The required identifiers are created during the ETL process. The fact table contains measurements from gas, energy and water meters. Some of them measure values in two separate zones. Such records are transformed into records containing one measured value each, with the zone number. The ETL process additionally creates a set of measurement groups; meters of the same type belonging to the same collecting node are put into the same group. Such a division is useful during analysis performed by the DSS system that uses the warehouse.

6.3   Extraction and Resumption Tests

The goal of the tests is to examine the influence of the balancing algorithm applied to our distributed warehouse system on the extraction process. We tested a pure Design-Resume resumption algorithm and a hybrid resumption, which is a combination of DR and staging technique. The tests base on the extraction graph presented in Sect. 6.1.

Comparing Figs. 9 and 10 one may conclude that the use of balancing has a marginally low influence on the performance of the extraction process. Of course we must not generalize: this takes place in our distributed warehouse system, where we have 5 machines acting as databases, and the extraction process is run on a single PC. The advantage of the balanced extraction does not exceed a few percentage points. Similarly there is no visible influence on the efficiency of the resumption process. However, the difference between pure DR and hybrid resumption is slightly bigger.

Looking at Fig. 11 we see that use of balancing makes the pure DR resumption more efficient than the case of unbalanced hybrid resumption. Of course,

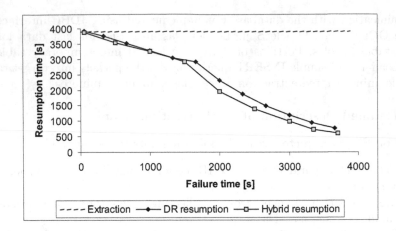

Fig. 9. Efficiency of resumption when fact table is uniformly distributed without balancing

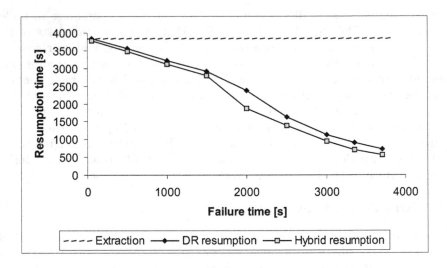

Fig. 10. Efficiency of resumption when fact table distribution relies on the balancing results

it does not take place in the whole range of the simulated failures. But for failures taking place before 1500 seconds of the extraction process, balanced DR resumption performs better. The situation rapidly changes after 1500 seconds (writing important part of stage data). From this moment on, balanced and unbalanced cases of both algorithms have a similar efficiency, with the balanced case enjoying a slight advantage.

In our opinion, the reason for such results is the single computer extraction process. It does not matter whether we balance the system. The system bottleneck during extraction is the PC running the extraction software. The other

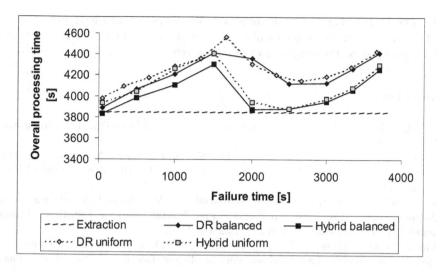

Fig. 11. Overall processing time as a function of the failure time. Overall processing time is the sum of resumption time and the time of failure. It expresses the time needed to ready the warehouse.

computers are fast enough to work efficiently even with unbalanced data. It is likely that, in order to take advantage of the balancing, the extraction must become a distributed process. This should preclude a single PC bottlenecking a whole system.

7   Summary

In the paper we focused on the influence of the data balancing used in our distributed warehouse system on the extraction and resumption processes performance. The Design-Resume algorithm [5] designed by Labio et al was briefly explained. This is the algorithm belonging to a group of redo algorithms. Its general idea was presented and its relatively few drawbacks were pointed out. We focused on the problem of resumption, when the extraction graph contains many loading nodes, and modified the algorithm to handle such cases more efficiently. An example of such a case was described in Sect. 6.1. The graph describes ETL process loading data to a distributed spatial data warehouse collecting telemetric measurements [3]. We examined a performance of the ETL process depending on the data distribution method. There were two possibilities: data distributed uniformly among system nodes according to the meter number, or balanced data distribution [4], where the balancing goal was to obtain the fastest response time of the system based on the warehouse.

As shown in the tests (Sect. 6.3), the influence of the balancing on the ETL process is very low. We observed reduction of the extraction process time by 1-2%. In our opinion, the reason for this is the single machine extraction process. In our tests the ETL software runs on one PC, and the 5 other PCs are warehouse system nodes running an Oracle database. We suspect that distributing the extraction process on the larger number of machines could bring more advantages. This is going to be the next step of our research.

References

1. Bruckner R., List B., Schiefer J.: Striving Towards Near Real-Time Data Integration for Data Warehouses. DaWaK 2002.
2. Galhardas H., Florescu D., Shasha D., Simon E.: Ajax: An Extensible Data Cleaning-Tool. In Proc. ACM SIGMOD Intl. Conf. On the Management of Data, Teksas (2000).
3. Gorawski M., Malczok R.: Distributed Spatial Data Warehouse Indexed with Virtual Memory Aggregation Tree. 5th Workshop on Spatial-Temporal DataBase Management (STDBM_VLDB'04), Toronto, Canada 2004.
4. Gorawski M., Chechelski R.: Spatial Telemetric Data Warehouse Balancing Algorithm in Oracle9i/Java Environment, Intelligent Information Systems, Gdansk, Poland, 2005.
5. Labio W., Wiener J., Garcia-Molina H., Gorelik V.: Efficient resumption of interrupted warehouse loads. SIGMOD Conference, 2000.
6. Labio W., Wiener J., Garcia-Molina H., Gorelik V.: Resumption algorithms. Technical report, Stanford University, 1998.
7. Sagent Technologies Inc.: Personal correspondence with customers.
8. Vassiliadis P., Simitsis A., Skiadopoulos S.: Modeling ETL Activities asGraphs. In Proc. 4th Intl. Workshop on Design and Management of Data Warehouses, Canada, (2002).
9. Vassiliadis P., Simitsis A., Georgantas P., Terrovitis M.: A Framework for the Design of ETL Scenarios. CAiSE 2003.

OLAP Schemata for Correct Applications

Hans-Joachim Lenz and Bernhard Thalheim

Free University Berlin, Institute of Production, Information Systems and Operations Research,
Garystr. 21, 14195 Berlin, Germany
Christian Albrechts University Kiel, Department of Computer Science and Applied
Mathematics, Olshausenstr. 40, D-24098 Kiel, Germany
hjlenz@wiwiss.fu-berlin.de, thalheim@is.informatik.uni-kiel.de

Abstract. OLAP applications are currently widely used in business applications. These applications are implicitly defined on top of OLTP systems. The applications make use of aggregation functions and data combinations. A number of paradoxes is observed if arbitrary aggregation functions and combinations are used. We develop a theory of aggregation functions, OLTP-OLAP transformations, and of the data cube. Based on these investigations we derive an *architecture for OLTP-OLAP applications* that supports sound and correct querying: OLTP-OLAP specification frames. The specification frame of OLTP-OLAP schemata specifically emphasises soundness of all operations involved by built-in guards. Or to turn it around, we make provision that an innocent user does not start non-sense operations. This specification frame is based on OLTP schemata, OLTP-OLAP transformations, and a rigid theory of OLAP schemata and functions.

1 Introduction

While OLTP systems are defined of a rigid mathematical way (e.g. [10]) OLAP systems lack so far of a rigid mathematical framework and of an engineering methodology for sound application. OLAP functionality is based on cube operations [4] that provide an intuitive way for data analysts to navigate through various levels of summary information in the data warehouse. In a data cube, attributes are categorized into dimension attributes and measure attributes. A number of pitfalls with respect to usage of OLAP databases [8, 6, 9] may happen when cube operations are executed. For example, OLAP operations are often not completely defined, the formal treatment of transformations within OLTP databases and OLAP operators is contradictive or consequences of inherent (stochastic) dependency structures between dimensions are unknown, and the innocent user does not know about implied side-effects.

Furthermore, a systematic treatment of OLTP-OLAP-transformations has not yet been developed. Thus, this paper extends [8, 6, 9] by providing a formal basis for OLAP schemata and for OLTP-OLAP transformations and by deriving a framework for sound OLAP applications.

[12] distinguishes three kinds of architecture: application architecture consisting of application modules, technical architecture that displays the overall (layered) structure of the modules, and architecture of technical infrastructure describing the technical systems architecture. We develop a proposal for a technical architecture of OLAP systems

D. Draheim and G. Weber (Eds.): TEAA 2005, LNCS 3888, pp. 99–113, 2006.

that is based on the OLTP-OLAP specification frame. This architecture support correctness of OLAP applications and provides guarantees for correct computations. For sake of convenience, we restrict the definitions to ER models [16].

2 The OLTP-OLAP Architecture

We define a layered OLTP-OLAP architecture by introducing an OLTP schema, by characterizing aggregations, and by introducing OLTP-OLAP transformations. Based on this framework we define the OLAP cube, OLAP query operations, and derive a specification frame that might be used for guaranteeing correctness of OLAP applications.

2.1 OLTP Schema

A database schema is based on a type system that is defined by the type definition

$$t = b \mid (A_1 : t_1, \ldots, A_n : t_n) \mid \{t\} \mid [t] \mid \ell : t$$

where ℓ is a collection of labels and b is an arbitrary collection of *base types*, e.g., base types such as $BOOL = \{\mathbf{T}, \mathbf{F}\}$, $\mathbb{1} = \{1\}$, $TEXT$, PIC, $MPIC$, $CARD$, INT, $REAL$, $DATE$, URL, and $MAIL$.

The union of all base types that are numeric is denoted by NUM. Confirming to conventions of database typing we use the labeled Cartesian product $(A_1 : t_1, \ldots, A_n : t_n)$ instead of property collection. Since we do not need cyclic types we restrict the type construction to rational trees [10].

This type system may be used to define ER-schemata through *hierarchical database types of level* k $E \stackrel{\circ}{=} (comp(E), attr(E), id(E))$ where E is the name of the type, $comp(E) = \{r_1 : E_1, \ldots, r_n : E_n\}$ are the component types of level less than k with pairwise different role names r_i and the set $attr(E) = \{A_1, \ldots, A_m\}$ of attributes is defined over domain types $dom(A_i)$, and $id(E)$ is a subset of $(comp(E) \cup attr(E)$ called primary identification.

An entity type is a type of level 0 and does not have any component types.

An *ER-cluster of level* k $frag(E) \stackrel{\circ}{=} \{f_1 : E_1, \ldots, f_n : E_n\}$ of fragments is defined with pairwise different fragment names f_i, database types (or clusters) E_i on levels at most k. We usually assume that at least one component type is of level $k - 1$ for each type of level at least 1. The domain types $dom(E)$ are defined through the type definition of E.

The *database schema* S consists of a finite set of database types and clusters and a set of integrity constraints Σ.

An *object* over $E = (comp(E), attr(E), id(E))$ is the partial mapping

$$t : comp(E) \cup attr(E) \rightarrow dom(E).$$

The *database* $\mathcal{DB}$ over a database schema S consists of a set of objects defined over types of $\mathcal{DB}$. We require that the set of objects for each type E is uniquely identified by their $id(E)$-values. Integrity constraints restrict the set of possible databases over S.

The first-order *query algebra* is defined with the basic functions projection (subtype function), union, product, difference, composition, abstraction, evaluation, selection, empty : $\mathbb{1} \rightarrow \{t\}$,   single : $t \rightarrow \{t\}$, equality predicate, membership, and triv : $t \rightarrow \mathbb{1}$.

General operations may be defined through structural recursion [1], for instance the SQL selection operation is defined by

$$\text{filter}(\varphi) = \text{src}[\emptyset, \text{if\_then\_else} \circ (\varphi \times \text{single} \times (\text{empty} \circ \text{triv})), \cup]$$

and the value transformation is defined through $\text{map}(f) = \text{src}[\emptyset, \text{single} \circ f, \cup]$.

Operations may lead to new types, e.g. the generalized join $t_1 \bowtie_t t_2$ defined the least common supertype t of t_1 and t_2. Operations can be based on identifiers, e.g. URI's.

Each query q of the query algebra has a type $type(q)$. A *view* V on $\mathcal{S}$ is given by defining query q_V that is defined over a view schema $\mathcal{S}_V$.

2.2 Classes of Aggregation Functions

We distinguish aggregation functions according to their computational complexity:

- The simplest class of aggregation functions use simple (one-pass) aggregation. A typical example are the simple statistical functions of SQL-92: *count (absolute frequency), average (arithmetic mean), sum (total), min, max.*
- More complex aggregation functions are used in cumulative or moving statistics which relate data subsets to other subsets or supersets, e.g. growth rates, changes in an aggregate value over time or any dimension set (banded reports, control break reports, OLAP dimensions). Typical examples are queries like:
  "What percentage each customer contributes to total sales?"
  "Total sales in each territory, ordered from high to low!"
  "Total amount of sales broken down by salesman within territories".

One can distinguish between distributive, algebraic and holistic aggregation functions:

Distributive or inductive functions are defined by structural recursion. Given types T, T' and a collection type C^T on T and operations such as generalized union $\cup_{C^T}$, generalized intersection $\cap_{C^T}$, and generalized empty elements $\emptyset_{C^T}$ on C^T and given further an element h_0 on T' and two functions defined on the types $h_1 \;:\; T \rightarrow T'$ and $h_2 \;:\; T' \times T' \rightarrow T'$,   then we define the structural recursion by insertion presentation for R^C on T as follows:
$$srec_{h_0,h_1,h_2}(\emptyset_{C^T}) := h_0$$
$$srec_{h_0,h_1,h_2}(\{\!|s|\!\}) := h_1(s) \qquad \text{for singleton collections } \{\!|s|\!\}$$
$$srec_{h_0,h_1,h_2}(R_1^C \cup_{C^T} \{\!|s|\!\}) := h_2(srec_{h_0,h_1,h_2}(R_1^C), h_1(s))$$
$$\text{iff } R_1^C \cap_{C^T} \{\!|s|\!\} = \emptyset_{C^T} .$$
Distributive functions preserve partitions of sets, i.e. given a set X and a partition $X = X_1 \cup X_2 \cup ... \cup X_n$ of X into pairwise disjoint subsets. Then for a distributive function f there exist a function g such that $f(X) = g(f(X_1), ..., f(X_n))$. Functions such as count, sum, min, max are distributive.

Algebraic functions can be expressed by finite algebraic expressions defined over distributive functions. Typical examples of algebraic functions in database languages are average and covariance. The average function for instance can be defined on the basis of an expression on count and sum.

Holistic functions are all other functions. For holistic functions there is no bound on the size of the storage needed to describe a sub-aggregate. Typical examples are `mostFrequent`, `rank` and `median` . Usually, their implementation and expression in database languages require tricky programming.

Holistic functions are computable over temporal views. We will not discuss these functions in detail within this paper.

2.3   OLTP-OLAP Transformations

OLTP-OLAP transformations are based on transforming functions

- a family of grouping functions $\mathcal{G}$,
- a family of aggregation functions $\mathcal{F}$, and
- a family of transformations $\mathcal{T}$.
  An example for a nonlinear transformation is the conversion of fuel consumption $\frac{l}{100km} \mapsto \frac{miles}{gallon}$ [5].

Since application frameworks require that properties must be provable we need a framework for OLTP-OLAP transformations too. This framework is based on the theory of aggregation functions introduced next.

In general, an aggregation function is definable as a specific family $\mathcal{F} = \{f_0, ..., f_k, ..., f_\omega\}$ with functions $f_k : Bag_k \to NUM$ that map a bag with k elements to a numerical range. A function f_k is called symmetric if $f_k(x_1, ..., x_k) = f_k(x_{\rho(1)}, ..., x_{\rho(k)})$ for any k-permutation ρ.

Definition 1. *A family of functions* $(f_k : Bag_k \to NUM|k \in \mathcal{N}_0)$ *for bags on* $dom(M)$ *is called* **aggregation function** *on M if they are monotone according to the order of* NUM, *symmetric, and each* f_k *is defined through structural recursion on the basis of* $f_1, ..., f_{k-1}$ *for* $k \geq 2$.

This definition is different from the definition given in [2]. We require associatedness within the family whereas [2] considers functions f_k on their own without relationship and additionally require boundedness. Aggregation functions from $\mathcal{F}$ may have the following properties:

Idempotent: $f_k(x, ..., x) = x$ for all $x \in NUM$,

Min/Max-invariant: $f_k(min, ..., min) = min$ and $f_k(max, ..., max) = max$ for the minimal and maximal elements in NUM,

Continuous: $\lim_{\underline{x}_i \to \underline{x}} f(\underline{x}_i) = f(\underline{x})$ for all vectores $\underline{x}_i, \underline{x}$ of size k,

Lipschitz property: $|f_k(x_1, ..., x_k) - f_k(y_1, ..., y_k)| \leq c \sum_{i=1}^{n} |x_i - y_j|$ for some constant c,

Self-identical: $f_k(x_1, ..., x_k) = f_{k+1}(x_1, ..., x_k, f_k(x_1, ..., x_k))$,

Shift-invariant: $f_k(x_1 + b, ..., x_k + b) = f_k(x_1, ..., x_k) + b$,

Homogeneous (of degree 1)*:* $f_k(bx_1, ..., bx_k) = bf_k(x_1, ..., x_k)$,

Additive: $f_k(x_1 + y_1, ..., x_k + y_k) = f_k(x_1, ..., x_k) + f_k(y_1, ..., y_k)$,

Associative: $f_r(f_{k_1}(\underline{x}_1), ..., f_{k_r}(\underline{x}_r)) = f_{k_1 + ... + k_r}(\underline{x}_1, ..., \underline{x}_r)$.

Proposition 1. *Aggregation functions have the following properties:*

`max`, `min` *are idempotent, min-/max-invariant, continuous, self-identical, additive, homogeneous, and associative and obey the Lipschitz property,*

sum *is continuous, homogeneous, additive, associative, obeys the Lipschitz property, and is not idempotent, not self-identical, not shift-invariant,*
avg *is idempotent, continuous, shift-invariant, homogeneous, additive, obeys the Lipschitz property, is not self-identical, not associative,*
count *is continuous, associative, obeys the Lipschitz property, not idempotent, not self-identical, not shift-invariant but cardinality preserving, not homogeneous, not additive but summarizable.*

The proof of the proposition is straight-forward and thus omitted.

Depending on these properties, the behavior of aggregation functions varies. For instance, if the aggregation function is not associative then roll-up may falsify the result.

The existence or the non-existence of null values in NUM is not only a design issue, but heavily influences the behavior of aggregation functions. For instance, as noted in [9] the min and max functions will not remain to be idempotent, the average function can be defined in at least nine different ways.

2.4   The Data Cube

The data cube [4] is a fundamental data structure of OLAP databases, and is known as multi-way table in Statistics. It is based on dimensional and measure (statistical) attributes. We develop a proper theory of the cube generalizing and extending the approach proposed by [16, 17].

Definition 2.   *Given for a type t and its domain dom(t).*
   - *A grouping L_i is defined on a set of selection expressions $\sigma_{\alpha_{i,1}}, ..., \sigma_{\alpha_{i,n_i}}$.*
   - *The grouping L_i is finer than L_j if either $\alpha_{i,k} \to \alpha_{j,l}$ or $(\alpha_{i,k} \wedge \alpha_{j,l}) \leftrightarrow 0$ for all $k(1 \leq k \leq n_i)$ and $l(1 \leq l \leq n_j)$. The trivial grouping is denoted by ALL.*
   - *The grouping L_i is a refinement of the grouping L_j ($L_i \preceq L_j$) if each group $g_{i,k}$ is subset of exactly one group $g_{j,l}$. In this case an anchoring function anc^{L_i,L_j} and a relation $desc^{L_i,L_j}$ that is inverse to anc^{L_i,L_j} are defined for each pair $L_i \preceq L_j$.*
   - *A hierarchically ordered dimension $\mathcal{D}$ consists of a type and a set of groupings $(\{L_1^{\mathcal{D}}, ..., L_n^{\mathcal{D}}, ALL\}, \preceq)$ that form a lattice.*
   - *Hierarchically ordered dimensions are well defined if all groupings form partitions (are pairwise disjoint and form a cover).*

According to [9] we consider only well-defined hierarchic dimensions in the sequel.

The time dimension is a typical example of a dimension. We use types *Seconds, Minutes, Hours, Days, Weeks, Months, Year* and the linear partial orders *Seconds* $\preceq$ *Minutes* $\preceq$ *Hours* $\preceq$ *Days* $\preceq$ *Months* $\preceq$ *Years, Days* $\preceq$ *Weeks, Weeks* $\not\preceq$ *Months, Weeks* $\not\preceq$ *Years,* where the function $anc^{\text{Minutes,Hours}}$ maps minutes (e.g. 10:02 am) to the hour they are embedded (e.g. 11 am). We may add also *FiscalDays, WorkingDays* etc.

Definition 3.   *A cube schema $C = (\mathcal{D}_1, ..., \mathcal{D}_m, M_1, ..., M_k, \Sigma_C)$ is given by*

   - *a set of well defined dimensions $\{\mathcal{D}_i | 1 \leq i \leq m\}$ that form a key of C,*
   - *a set of fact attributes $M_1, ... M_k$, an associated set of aggregation functions $\mathcal{F}$, and a set of associated transformations $t_1, ..., t_k \in \mathcal{T}$, and*
   - *a set of integrity constraints Σ_C.*

Definition 4. *A cube algebra is given by*

- *a cube schema C and*
- *an algebra consisting of at least navigation, selection, projection and split functions.*

In the sequel we show that cube operations must be applied and used with care and with full understanding of the semantic and statistical properties of the data taken from a given application domain. Moreover, they must be equal in all respects with the objectives of the corresponding decision making.

2.5 OLAP Query Operations

We introduce now the main query operations. Selection is based on a criterion that is evaluated against data or levels of dimension in order to restrict the set of retrieved data. Roll-up is an aggregation of data from a lower level to a higher level of granularity within a dimensions hierarchy. Drill-down is the inverse of roll-up. Dice can be defined by roll-up to ALL. Slice groups data with respect to a proper subset of dimensions of a cube. The last four operations may be considered to be navigation operations. Thus, the data cube is mainly queried by selection and navigation.

More formally, the following basic OLAP query functions are introduced for a cube $C = \{(d_1, ..., d_m, m_1, ..., m_k)\}$ defined on the cube schema $(\mathcal{D}_1, ..., \mathcal{D}_m, M_1, ..., M_k, \Sigma_C)$, a dimension $\mathcal{D}$, the lattice $(\{L_1^{\mathcal{D}}, ..., L_n^{\mathcal{D}}, ALL\}, \preceq)$:

Basic drill-down functions are used for decomposing groups of data along a well-defined dimension $\mathcal{D}$. Given two groupings $L_i \succeq L_i'$ of $\mathcal{D}$. The values for the fact values on $M_1, ..., M_k$ are obtained through $anc^{L_i, L_i'}$ by decomposition. We obtain the cube $C' = \{(d_1, ..., d_m, m_1'', ..., m_k'')\}$ that is bound to C by the condition $m_j' = \sum_{(d_i, d_i) \in anc^{L_i, L_i'}, (d_1, ..., d_i', ..., l_m, .-, ..., m_j'', .-, ...,) \in C'} m_j''$.
We observe that the corresponding aggregation functions must be additive along $L_i \succeq L_i'$.

Basic dice functions are similar to projection in the first-order query algebra. Given a dimension $\mathcal{D}_i$. The projection $C' = \pi_{\mathcal{D}_1, ..., \mathcal{D}_{i-1}, \mathcal{D}_{i+1}, ..., \mathcal{D}_m}(C)$ computes the cube C' with objects $(d_1, ..., d_{i-1}, d_{i+1}, ..., d_m, m_1', ..., m_k',) \in C'$ such that $m_j' = \sum_{(d_1, ..., d_m, m_1, ..., m_k) \in C} m_j$ for all $j (1 \le j \le k)$.
We observe that the corresponding aggregation functions must be additive along $L_i \succeq L_i'$.

Basic slice functions similar to selection of tuples within a set. Given a dimension $\mathcal{D}_i$ and a set V of values v with the granularity of $L_i^{\mathcal{D}}$, i.e. such values v for which $desc^{ALL, L_i}$ is defined. The cube $\delta_V(C)$ consists of those objects $(d_1, ..., d_m, m_1, ..., m_k) \in C$ for which $d_i \in V$.

Basic roll-up functions are the opposite of the basic drill-down functions, i.e. for given L_i, L_i' with $L_i \preceq L_i'$, for the cube C, for $M_1, ..., M_k$ and $desc^{L_i, L_i'}$ we obtain the cube $C' = \{(d_1', ..., d_m', m_1', ..., m_k')\}$ that is bound to C by the condition $m_j' = \sum_{(d_i, d_i') \in desc^{L_i, L_i'}, (d_1, ..., d_i', ..., d_m, .-, ..., m_j, .-, ...,) \in C} m_j$.
We observe that the relationship $desc^{L_i, L_i'}$ must be disjoint within the cube C along $L_i \succeq L_i'$.

These operations may be combined using staggering of functions. We, thus, obtain drill-down functions by superposing drill-down functions. Generalizing the first-order query algebra, [16] defines additional OLAP operations such as

join functions for mergers of cubes,
union functions for union of two or more cubes of identical type,
rotation or pivoting functions for rearrangement of the order of dimensions, and
rename functions for renaming of dimensions.

We observe:

Proposition 2. *The slice, drill-down, roll-up, union, rotate, and rename functions form a relationally complete query algebra of OLAP operations.*

The proof is based on the relational completeness of the corresponding operations of the first-order query algebra.

2.6 The OLTP-OLAP Specification Frame

We already observed that the correctness of computations within the cube depends on the aggregations and OLAP query functions, and on properties of the domains of fact attributes $M_1, ..., M_k$. If we do not need all OLAP query functions then correctness of computation may be achieved more easily. If some of the aggregation functions are not of interest in the given application we may exclude them. The domain types of the fact attributes M_j may preserve a set Ψ of properties. Furthermore, the correctness depends on the cube under consideration. Therefore, we propose specification frames restricting OLAP applications.

Various modeling assumptions can be applied to cubes:

- **Disjointness:** OLTP-OLAP transformations are restricted to groupings which generate disjoint groups.
- **Completeness:** Groupings used for OLTP-OLAP transformations cover the entire set of database objects.
- **$\mathcal{P}$-subset invariance:** Fact values are stable if the OLTP database is restricted to objects based on the policy $\mathcal{P}$.
- **$\mathcal{P}$-union invariance:** Fact values are stable if the OLTP database is extended by new objects depending on the policy $\mathcal{P}$.
- **Equidistance:** Used transformations $T \in \mathcal{T}$ are linear.

A policy restricts the modification of a database. Policies are used to automatically enforce OLTP and OLAP constraints integrity. Integrity enforcement is based on the constraints management supported by systems (checking mode, statement or row level, pre- or postconditions, scope conditions, matching conditions, reference types), integrity constraint modules execution (scheduling, conflict resolution, and granularity of triggers or procedures; order of execution), level of consistency during integrity control, and level of specification (declarative, imperative, interface-backed).

Domain types may be restricted by properties such as precision and accuracy, granularity, and ordering. Furthermore, domains can be based on scales, can represent classifications and can contain default values and neutral values. Domain values can be extended by measures, e.g., relative, absolute, linear and non-linear. Domain values can be transformed by casting functions to values of other domain types. [16] distinguishes nominal, absolute, rank, ratio, atomar, complex, and interval types.

Definition 5. *A* **specification frame** $\mathfrak{F} = (\mathfrak{A}, \mathfrak{O}, \Psi, \mathfrak{M})$ *consists of a set* $\mathfrak{A}$ *of aggregation functions under consideration, a set* $\mathfrak{O}$ *of OLAP query operations, a set* Ψ *of properties, and a set* $\mathfrak{M}$ *of modeling assumptions.*

The cube C *is called* $\mathfrak{F}$-**correct** *if the OLTP-OLAP transformations are restricted to the functions in* $\mathfrak{A}$*, fact domains fulfill* Ψ*, and the modeling assumptions are valid for the cube* C.

Definition 6. *An* **OLAP schema** *is based on an OLTP schema* S *and on a specification frame* $\mathfrak{F}$ *and consists of a set of* $\mathfrak{F}$-correct cubes.

Next we show how to avoid incorrect application cases. Then we characterize OLAP schemata by elaborating modeling assumptions.

3   Incorrect OLAP Applications and Their Properties

3.1   Summarization over a One-Way Table

The first category of problematic OLAP applications is related to grouping [8].

Proposition 3. *Roll-up operations becomes incorrect if hierarchies used for the cube are not based on the disjointness property for groupings.*

The proof of this observation is straightforward.

3.2   The Simpson Paradox

Our next example leads into problems caused by cube operator 'dicing'(margining). Consider an example given in [4] as an example for well-designed cube on 'counts of sold cars grouped by model, color, and year' with slightly changed numbers:

Table 1. count $(*)$ by model, color, year (data under a join dependency, i.e. MVD)

model	Chevy				Ford				ALL
color	blue		white		blue		white		ALL
year	90	91	90	91	90	91	90	91	ALL
count	255	156	88	82	174	102	222	175	1254

We can compute the following percentage from Table 1:

$$p(\text{chevy}|\text{blue}, 90) \quad \approx \quad 59\%, \quad p(\text{chevy}|\text{blue}, 91) \quad \approx \quad 60\%$$

We observe that the market share of a blue car of type 'chevy' increases slightly over years 90 - 91. The increase of the share is stronger for white cars:

$$p(\text{chevy}|\text{white}, 90) \quad \approx \quad 28\%, \quad p(\text{chevy}|\text{white}, 91) \quad \approx \quad 32\%$$

If we dice in Table 1 over 'color', we get:

$$p(\text{chevy}, 90) \approx 46\%, \quad p(\text{chevy}, 91) \approx 46\%.$$

Evidently, the dicing operator may lead to contradictory results! This spurious effect is called Simpson Paradox [13]. This happens if one dices or summarizes over a separator Z of a binary join dependency which is a type of MVD $Z \twoheadrightarrow X|Y$ or binary join dependency $\bowtie (XZ, YZ)$ of a relational scheme with attribute set $X \cup Y \cup Z$.

We summarize this subsection by an observation that is obvious.

Proposition 4. *Dice or roll-up operations become incorrect if multivalued dependencies are not preserved.*

3.3   Non-commutative Operators

The following example is taken from [5]. Consider the Table 2 that provides a basis for decisions of two investors, I_G and I_{UK}, whether to buy car A or B based only on a nation-wide investment criterion, i.e. car economy or fuel consumption efficiency[1]. The

Table 2. Economy Indicators of three cars A,B, C compiled for two investors from Germany (col. 3) and Great Britain (col.4)

Car Type	Area	Consumption Rate l/100 km	Range mi/gal
A	City	16	14.7
	Country	4	58.8
	Overall Mean	**10**	**36.7**
B	City	8	29.4
	Country	8	29.4
	Overall Mean	**8**	**29.4**
C	City	20	11.8
	Country	6	39.2
	Overall Mean	**13**	**25.5**

cube in Table 2 represents the statistics 'total efficiency' (consumption rate and range) or 'mean efficiency' by car type and area: Investor I_G will prefer car B as the investment object with minimum mean consumption, while investor and I_{UK}, will vote for car A as the winner due to a maximum range! The different decisions based on different decision making criteria will disappear if cars A and C are compared. In this case, the data of the cube lead both investors to the same decision even if they use their own decision criteria.

Evidently, the investors in UK and D make coherent decisions based on the same database as before! Why leads data analysis sometimes to contradictory results? The answer is straightforward when one considers the operations involved in Table 2. The involved transformation or mapping f : numeric $\rightarrow$ numeric is non-linear, i.e. $r' = f(r) = \frac{c}{r}$ with $c = \frac{378.54118}{1.609344} \approx 235.2$. The second operation

---

[1] Note, that the conditions of the tests are made comparable, i.e. same distances travelled in Germany and same number of Gallons filled up for the rides in UK for both areas.

involved is the arithmetic mean or average (avg), which is a linear mapping of type mean : numeric $\times$ numeric $\rightarrow$ numeric and is defined by $avg(v1, v2) = \frac{v1+v2}{2}$. Remember now the following

Theorem 1 (Non commutative operators). *Let* **O** *be a given set of numeric operators. Let* $o_1 \in$ **O** *be a linear operator and* $o_2 \in$ **O** *a non-linear operator. Then it is generally not true that* $o_1 \circ o_2 = o_2 \circ o1$. *In other words, the operators* o_1 *and* o_2 *are not commutative.*

Theorem 1 explains that transformation f and the arithmetic mean are not generally inter-changeable. This fact is essential even in the phase of popularization of a data warehouse as part of ETL (Extraction-Transformation-Loading).

3.4 Perfect Aggregation

Our next example is related to linear economic aggregation theory. Its beginning is due to [3]. We consider N households and their data on monthly income and expenditures over G months. The question arises whether it is feasible first to aggregate the data across the N households and then to establish a time-invariant linear regression consumption model between expenditures and income per month. Alternatively, is it feasible to start with N consumption models of expenditures and income for each household first and then to aggregate over G months? Our main message is disappointing for cube materialisation: There exists an appropriate homomorphism H only if a pseudo-inverse of the aggregations are used [3, 11, 15] and [7].

Consider the following linear micro model $\underline{y} = \underline{A}\,\underline{x}$, where $\underline{y}' = (Y_1, Y_2, ..., Y_G)$ $\in R^G$ is a vector of monthly expenditures of a household, $\underline{x}'$ is a corresponding vector of monthly income[2] The homomorphism diagram in Figure 1 illustrates this evaluation procedure.

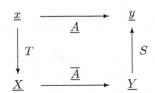

Fig. 1. Homomorphism diagram illustrating Theorem 2

Let $T : R^H \rightarrow R^J$ (J $\leq$ H) be a linear aggregation function with $\underline{X} = T\underline{x}$. The corresponding macro model is $\underline{Y} = \overline{A}X$ with $\underline{Y}' = (Y_1, Y_2, ..., Y_F)$. We define the statistic $\underline{S} : R^F \rightarrow R^G$, and one gets $\hat{\underline{y}} = SY$.

Definition 7 (Perfect (linear) Aggregation). *The aggregation (S, T) is called perfect iff* $\hat{\underline{y}} = \underline{y}$.

The existence of a perfect aggregation is assured by the following theorem.

---

[2] Notice, that we do not include errors in the equation for the sake of simplified presentation.

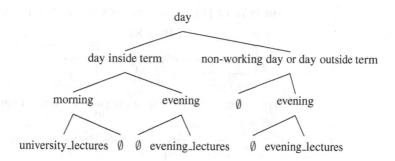

Fig. 2. Example of a collapsing hierarchy which prohibit roll-ups

Theorem 2 (Existence of a perfect aggregation). *The perfect homomorphism*

$$H : \hat{\underline{y}} = \underline{y} \quad \text{exists if and only if} \quad \hat{y} = \underline{S}\overline{A}T$$

for $\overline{A} = \underline{S}^{+}\underline{A}T^{+}$ *where* $\underline{S}^{+}(T^{+})$ *is the Moore-Penrose inverse of* $\underline{S}(T)$.

The theorem implies that an aggregation becomes incorrect if and only if the matrix $\overline{A}$ is not used.

3.5 The Cube Operator in Collapsing Hierarchies

We close with an example from [9]. The day hierarchy (classification) in Figure 2 is asymmetric and unbalanced. Such hierarchies may collapse whenever groups are combined without preservation of the asymmetry. The inhomogeneous granularity of attributes involved causes an in-coherency of information computed by the cube operator.

We observe that there exist a (dangerous) collapsing hierarchy, because no morning lectures are given on non-working days. In such cases special attention must be paid to a roll-up crossing various levels of the classification tree, and SQL queries concerning different sub-trees, for instance reasoning on weak functional dependencies as defined by [6]. The following observation is easy to prove.

Proposition 5. *Summarization may become incorrect if hierarchies are collapsing or the completeness modeling assumption is not preserved.*

3.6 Loss of Identification in OLTP Schemata

Snodgrass uses in his book [14] an example that we can use for illustration of loss of identification. He uses the cube in Figure 3 for development of temporal formula. The data behind the cube must use, however, the entity type *Cattle*.

The schema may be used for *Pen-Lot* management. [14] demonstrates that history tracking and application of roll-up, dice or slice functions lead to OLAP queries that are very difficult to express through SQL. We may use this example to derive another modeling assumption:

Proposition 6. *Algebraic and holistic aggregation functions cannot be correctly used if identification of objects is lost.*

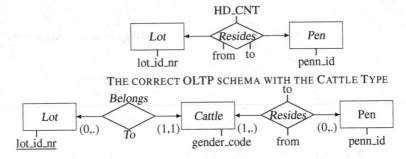

THE CUBE OF [14] AGGREGATED OVER THE CATTLE TYPE

THE CORRECT OLTP SCHEMA WITH THE CATTLE TYPE

Fig. 3. Example of an Identity Loss

4 Asserting Correctness

4.1 Properties of Aggregation Functions

The above presented observations may lead to the conclusion not to use the cube operator at all. We use them however for deriving correctness conditions for OLAP schemata.
On the basis of structural recursion we can prove a positive result for OLAP query operations:

Theorem 3. *Distributive aggregation functions are invariant for dice, roll-up, and
drill-down aggregation operations.*

This property is not valid neither for algebraic nor for holistic aggregation functions.

Definition 8. *Given a query function q, a database $\mathcal{DB}$, and an aggregation function
$f \in \mathcal{F}$. The function q is called $\mathcal{F}$-invariant in $\mathcal{DB}$ if $f(q(\mathcal{DB})) = g(\mathcal{DB})$ for appropriate $f, g \in \mathcal{F}$.*

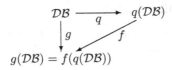

Fig. 4. Invariance of functions for transformations

We may directly conclude the following properties:

Corollary 1. *Roll-up functions are neither sum-invariant nor avg-invariant in general.*

Corollary 2. *Roll-up functions are not min- or max-invariant in general.*

Corollary 3. *Rearrangement functions are min-, max-, count-, sum- and avg-invariant.*

4.2   Correctness Conditions

Incorrectness does not appear in any case. Cube operations may be still correct for some data, whereas in other cases incorrectness becomes obvious. The development of guidelines is a appropriate way to avoid incorrectness. We may include these guidelines into the specification of OLAP schemata depending on the functions used. We use the theorems, propositions and conclusions of previous sections and derive a number of observations:

Drill-down functions are used for decomposing groups of data along a hierarchy.
Observation 1.
Drill-down functions are well defined if the cube construction is based on disjointness and completeness modeling assumptions.

Observation 2.
Drill-down functions are well defined if data granularity is guaranteed at leaf level L_1 and no structural null are used at any level L_i ($i > 1$) in between.

Roll-up functions are used for merging groups along a hierarchy. Problematic results are observed for collapsing hierarchies especially in the case of algebraic and holistic aggregation functions.
We consider groups $g_{p,1}, ...g_{p,s}$ and $g_{r,1}, ..., g_{r,t}$ of levels $L_p \preceq L_r$. Let $G_i = \{g \in L_p | anc(g) = g_{r,i}\}$. Groups at level p may fulfill a property α. The summarization over a fact attribute for all members of a group g is denoted by $o(g)$.
Observation 3.
The Simpson paradox is observed if for groups at level $L_p \preceq L_r$
$$(o(\sigma_\alpha(G_i)) < o(\sigma_\alpha(G_k)) \neq o(g_{r,i}) < o(g_{r,k})$$

Observation 4.
Roll-up functions are only well-defined if data granularity (i.e. value identifiability) is guaranteed at leaf level L_1 and no structural null are used at any level L_i ($i > 1$) in between.

Observation 5.
Roll-up functions must be query-invariant, i.e. for the roll-up function o and the query function q: $q(\bar{x}_1, ...\bar{x}_n) = q(o(\bar{x}_1), ..., o(\bar{x}_n))$.

Observation 6.
Roll-up functions must be based on disjointness and completeness modeling assumptions.

Dice functions are similar to projection, similar to marginalization in statistics, and similar to summing up unions of values. They are unproblematic for distributive functions. Algebraic aggregation functions may be combined with repairing functions[9].
Observation 7.
The Simpson paradox is observed if for groups at level $L_p \preceq L_r$
$$(o(\sigma_\alpha(G_i)) < o(\sigma_\alpha(G_k)) \neq o(g_{r,i}) < o(g_{r,k})$$

Observation 8.
Dice functions can only correctly be applied if the cube construction is based on union invariance, i.e. $\mathfrak{F}(\bigsqcup^*_{o \in g_i} value(o)) = \bigsqcup^*_{o \in g_i} (\mathfrak{F}(value(o)))$ for groups g_i for the generalized union $\bigsqcup^*$.
If $\mathfrak{F}$ is distributive then the $\bigsqcup^* \equiv \mathfrak{F}$. If $\mathfrak{F}$ is algebraic then repair functions must be applied.

Observation 9.
Dice functions can only be used along dimensions for which constraints among cube dimensions are not lost, i.e. if the constraint set that is shrinked to the new dimensions implies all constraints within these new dimensions.

Observation 10.
Dice functions must be based on disjointness and completeness modeling assumptions.

Slice functions are similar to selection of tuples within a set. They are subset operation and equivalent to conditioning in statistics.

Observation 11.
Slice functions must be query-invariant, i.e. for the slice function o'' and the query function q: $q(\underline{x}_1, ... \underline{x}_n) = q(o''(\underline{x}_1), ..., o''(\underline{x}_n))$.

Observation 12.

Slice functions must be subset invariant.

Constraints invalidated by subset construction are those integrity constraints that have to be expressed through $\forall\exists$-constraints[16], e.g., inclusion dependencies, multivalued dependencies, tuple-generating constraints.

OLTP-OLAP transformations can cause paradoxes or lead to problematic OLAP schemes. Statistics and the theory of mathematical functions have developed a rich theory, e.g., [2], that must be considered for OLTP-OLAP transformations. The arithmetic average is very sensitive to extreme values such as outliers and may be distorted by them.

Observation 13.
Application of median instead of mean average functions for aggregation leads to a robust OLAP query operation.

Observation 14.
Harmonic mean functions $\frac{n}{\sum_{i=1}^{n} \frac{1}{x_i}}$ are shift-invariant, additive, symmetric, continuous, and homogeneous.

Note, if we use this mean in Table 2, all three comparisons will become coherent.

Observation 15.
Geometric mean functions $\sqrt[n]{x_1 \cdot x_2 \cdot ... \cdot x_n}$ provide a better picture for relative scales among values and are OLAP query invariant.

5   Conclusion

This paper demonstrates how OLAP applications must be restricted by constraints in order to guarantee correctness of OLAP query operations. We introduced the OLTP-OLAP transformations and propose a mathematical definition of cubes that allows to define the classical OLAP query operations. Based on these definitions we introduce OLTP-OLAP specification frames that should become part of an OLAP repository. We demonstrate the power of the approach by revisiting paradoxes of OLAP computations and by deriving properties that provide correctness of of OLAP computations. The OLTP-OLAP specification frame can be considered as a specific layered (technical) architecture that allows to correctly reason in OLAP applications.

References

1. P. Buneman, L. Libkin, D. Suciu, V. Tannen, and L. Wong. Comprehension syntax. *SIGMOD Record*, 23(1):87–96, 1994.
2. T. Calvo, G. Mayor, and R. Mesiar. *Aggregation operators - New trends and applications.* Physica, Heidelberg, 2002.
3. W. D. Fisher. Optimal aggregation in multi-equation prediction models. *Econometrica*, 30:744–769, 1962.
4. J. Gray, S. Chaudhuri, A. Bosworth, A. Layman, D. Reichart, and M. Venkatrao. Data cube: A relational aggregation operator generalizing group-by, cross-tab, and sub-totals. *Data Mining and Knowledge Discovery*, 1(1):29–53, 1997.
5. D. J. Hand. Deconstructing statistical questions (with discussion). *Journal of the Royal Statistical Society, Series A*, 157:317–356, 1994.
6. W. Lehner, J. Albrecht, and H. Wedekind. Normal forms for multivariate databases. In *SSDBM X, Capri*, 1998.
7. H.-J. Lenz. Contribution to the discussion on "Deconstructing statistical questions" by David J. Hand. Read before The Royal Statistical Society , London, Dec 15th 1993.
8. H.-J. Lenz and A. Shoshani. Summarizability in OLAP and statistical databases. In *SSDBM IX, 1997, Washington*, 1997.
9. H.-J. Lenz and B. Thalheim. OLAP Databases and Aggregation Functions. In *Proc. 13th Intern. Conf. on Scientific and Statistical Database Management, Jul 18-20, 2001, George Mason University, Fairfax, Virginia, USA*, pages 91–100. IEEE Computer Society, 2001.
10. K.-D. Schewe and B. Thalheim. Fundamental concepts of object oriented databases. *Acta Cybernetica*, 11(4):49–81, 1993.
11. H. Schneeweiß. Das Aggregationsproblem. *Statistische Hefte*, 6:1–26, 1965.
12. J. Siedersleben. *Moderne Softwarearchitektur.* dpunkt-Verlag, 2004.
13. C. H. Simpson. The interpretation of interaction in contingency tables. *JRSS, series B*, 13:238–241, 1951.
14. R. T. Snodgrass. *Developing time-oriented database applications in SQL.* Morgan Kaufmann, San Francisco, 1999.
15. D. Sondermann. Optimale Aggregation von großen Gleichungssystemen. *Zeitschrift für Nationalökonomie*, 33:235–250, 1973.
16. B. Thalheim. *Entity-relationship modeling – Foundations of database technology.* Springer, Berlin, 2000.
17. P. Vassiladis and S. Skiadopooulos. Modeling and optimization issues for multidimensional databases. In *Proc. CAiSE'2000*, LNCS 1789, pages 482–497. Springer, Berlin.

Towards a Secure Data Stream Management System

Wolfgang Lindner[1] and Jörg Meier[2]

[1] MIT, Cambridge,
MA, USA
wolfgang@csail.mit.edu
[2] University Erlangen-Nuremberg
Erlangen, Germany
sijomeie@stud.uni-erlangen.de

Abstract. Todays data stream management systems (DSMSs) lack security functionality. Based on adversary scenarios we show how a DSMS architecture can be protected. We sketch a general DSMS architecture and introduce security issues that need to be considered. To face the threats we develop an extended system architecture that provides the necessary security mechanisms. We descuss the chosen concepts and illustrate how they can be realized by various system components. Our design focus is, considering the unique properties of data stream engines, to keep the impact on existing system components as little as possible and to limit the effect on the overall performance to a minimum.

1 Introduction

Data Stream Management Systems (DSMSs) have been developed over the past several years. The focus of research was on query processing and optimization [2], distribution [9] and most recently integration of data sources [3]. Security issues have not been addressed.

DSMSs differ from existing systems such as database management systems (DBMSs) in many aspects. For instance users run continuous queries which produce results by processing a continuous data stream. Without proper security mechanisms users have access to the entire system, including the ability to view and modify its behavior, data, and queries.

Because of this lack we focus in this paper on how to secure DSMSs based on the unique properties of such systems. Next, we introduce some scenarios which show the way a DSMS is used normally. In a second step we illustrate possible attacks to an unprotected DSMS.

As an example consider a DSMS that processes stock prices. It receives the changing share prices as an input data stream and executes queries of different customers based on that information. A company providing this system gets paid for delivering the results to its customer's queries. We can describe the way users work with the system by the following use cases.

D. Draheim and G. Weber (Eds.): TEAA 2005, LNCS 3888, pp. 114–128, 2006.

An administrator sets the system up, connects certain data sources containing stock price information, and supervises the system while it is running. The operation company might want to integrate different data sources from certain information providers. These sources delivering streamed data have to be attached to the system. Based on the agreement between a certain customer and the operating company the administrator ensures that the user is able to perform the tasks he paid for. A customer connects to the system with a client application, browses through the available data sources, inserts queries to the DSMS, receives the results, and uses them. A customer might want to change a query to get different results or to adjust the running query. He might also insert additional queries or delete existing ones. Customers might store certain query results in the system for later analysis, e.g., the average price each day for certain shares.

Now imagine an adversary attacking such a system without proper security mechanisms. We consider the following scenarios:

1. The adversary connects to the system and (a) sees all available data sources and possibly (b) the internal state of the system disclosing the other users' identities and their operations including the results. The malicious user can infer from that information strategies and possible plans of competitors.
2. Not only by connecting directly to the system the adversary can read "confidential" data, but also by intercepting the connection of the output stream to other clients.
3. The adversary can modify data by inserting certain operators into the query graph. Another customer might therefore get incorrect stock prices and make decisions which may cause financial damage.
4. In addition, it is possible that the adversary (a) fakes the incoming data before it reaches the DSMS by changing it at any point in the network which the data passes. Also, he could (b) pretend to be a certain information supplier and deliver incorrect or even malicious source data.
5. A malicious user can perform unauthorized tasks. For example, (a) using certain operators for data processing without having permission. That also includes (b) administrative actions like changing certain settings or even shutting down the whole system.
6. An attacker could claim to be a certain customer and perform actions on behalf of that customer, e. g. deleting stored data, changing or quitting running queries. Again, that could cause financial damage to the real customer who uses the results.
7. An adversary could fully load the system by performing queries that consume the whole available system capacity, e. g. in terms of computational power. He might also increase his queries' priorities so that the queries of other customers can not deliver results in time.

According to [7, 15], these adversary scenarios can be clustered into three threat categories. We associate the described scenarios with the following categories:

(C1) *Improper release of information*, which can be further divided into
  (C1a) *disclosure of data* [scenarios 1a, 2] (either inside the query network or while transferring it over the network) and
  (C1b) *disclosure of system internals* [scenario 1b].
(C2) *Improper modification of data*, where we distinguish between
  (C2a) *changes outside the system* [scenarios 4a, 4b] (before the input stream reaches the system or after the output stream leaves the system) and
  (C2b) *changes inside the query network* [scenarios 3, 5a, 6] (either the streaming data or the query graph).
(C3) *Denial of service attacks* [scenarios 5b, 7]

In this paper we address all of these problems. After sketching a general DSMS architecture in Sect. 3, we briefly describe common security aspects that need to be considered in Sect. 4. We address the illustrated security problems with proper solutions in Sect. 5. We show how the introduced mechanisms can be integrated into the architecture.

2   Related Work

As far as we know, none of the current DSMSs provides security. The following projects are examples for such data stream processing engines.

Borealis [1], an existing prototype, which is been developed at Brandeis University, Brown University, and MIT, is based on *Aurora* [2] and *Medusa* [16]. Aurora* is a distributed version of Aurora while Medusa is a federated distributed system. Many of the ideas in Borealis are developed in these two projects. These prototypes use a XML description for schema and queries in a box-and-arrow semantic. *STREAM* [4] or the STanford stREam datA Manager is supposed to be a "general-purpose" DSMS and is a project of Stanford University. To express queries, a language called CQL (Continuous Query Language) is introduced. Declarative queries are compiled into a query plan. *PIPES* [12] is a project of the University of Marburg using a "hybrid multi-threaded scheduling" three layer architecture. *TelegraphCQ* [8], a general system for adaptive data flow processing with an extension to support shared continuous queries, is a project developed at Berkeley University.

3   Background

To propose solutions for securing DSMSs we briefly sketch a general data stream architecture. Next, we discuss security issues that have to be considered.

Our general architecture of a data stream processing system (ignoring distribution [9] and high availability [10]) is shown in Fig. 1. We derived the illustrated architecture mainly from the mentioned prototypes and research projects [16, 4, 12, 8].

We differentiate between user-interaction with the system, which is shown on the top right of Fig. 1, and administrative actions which take place on the top left.

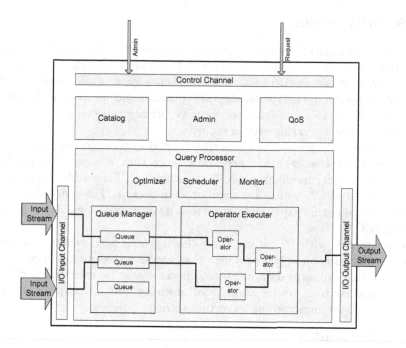

Fig. 1. Common DSMS Architecture

The latter includes management tasks like connecting or disconnecting streams. Every request reaches the system through the CONTROL CHANNEL. The QUERY PROCESSOR (QP) is the core of the system. The actual transformation of the incoming data stream (via the I/O INPUT CHANNEL) is done there by combining operator-boxes, executing them in the OPERATOR EXECUTER and, finally, streaming the results to the I/O OUTPUT CHANNEL. The query optimization process is controlled by the OPTIMIZER and is supported by the SCHEDULER and the MONITOR. Queues are managed by the QUEUE MANAGER. They are able to provide views on data streams as well as temporarily store data for window based operations. Queues can also be used between two operator-boxes. The ADMIN module controls the system, especially the QP. Every control interaction with the system is managed here. The QoS component keeps track of the overall system performance and the adherence to given QoS-requirements. The CATALOG stores meta-data and query diagram descriptions. It is accessible by all components. The CATALOG is consulted when a user wants to access objects in the system.

In the future the described architecture can be extended with a database attached to the DSMS. In this way persistently stored data can be processed together with streaming data and users are able to save information, e.g. calculated results (as an example see the use cases in Sect. 1). This extension enables the DSMS to provide the user with a service which includes traditional data management (like in DBMSs) together with stream processing capabilities. However, we do not consider this scenario due to the limited space here.

4   Security Issues

Securing an information system in general involves different security issues. To reach the three major security goals, which are confidentiality, integrity and availability, different mechanisms exist: Authentication, authorization and access control, auditing, encryption, digital signatures and message authentication codes. We will not focus on inference security, privacy aspects, physical or hardware security, nor operating system security.

Next, we briefly present the concepts behind *authentication, authorization and access control*, as well as *encryption*, since they are essential for implementing any security mechanism and data protection. They address the security categories C1 and C2, which are introduced in Sect. 1. The remaining aspects are out of scope of this paper and not further investigated. *Availability* is related to category C3.

In accordance with [7] we use the following terms: A *subject* is a user or programs that runs on behalf of a user that accesses the system. Any entity in the system that contains data or allows operations to be executed is called an *object*. *Access controls* are responsible for ensuring that all subjects access the objects in the system according to certain security policies.

4.1   Authentication

In order to distinguish between different identities (subjects), we need to *authenticate*. Authentication is any process by which the system verifies that someone is who he claims he is. This usually involves a username and a password, but can include any other method of demonstrating identity, such as biometric attributes [7]. Authentication measures can be distinguished between knowledge, possession and biometrics. The unique identification of subjects is the basis of every further authorization mechanism.

4.2   Authorization

Once a user is identified, the *authorization* process has to decide if the subject is permitted to access a certain resource (object) [7]. This is usually determined by finding out if that person is a part of a particular group, if that person has paid admission, has a particular level of security clearance, or has certain access rights. Authorization is based on access control, which consists of access rights and control policies.

4.3   Access Control

Access Control ensures that every access to the system occurs according to certain security rules. That involves different aspects: Access Rights, Access Matrix and Control Policies and other issues like Quality of Service and Time-based access. We illustrate them in the following paragraphs.

Access Rights. In [13] a reference for database access rights is given based on the SQL99 standard: *grant, revoke, select, insert, delete, references, update, grant* *o*ption, *create*, and *drop*. Commercial database systems like Oracle or Microsoft SQL-Server distinguish several of these access rights. We briefly describe the most important ones:

- **Select.** The data in the system can be read. That includes the meta data (e.g. the schema) about an accessed object.
- **Insert.** Data can be added and saved persistently.
- **Delete.** Stored Data can be deleted.
- **Grant option.** Access rights can be passed to other subjects.
- **References.** The right to define foreign keys.
- **Create, Alter, Drop.** Creating, changing or deleting the schema.
- **Grant, Revoke.** The permission to change access rights.

Access Matrix and Control Policies. Once a subject is authorized (or a process running on behalf of users), we want to determine whether or not the given identity is allowed to access a resource. Thus we need to implement a relation between subjects and objects with certain access rights. As described in [14] there are two different concepts to implement an access matrix that will establish the connection between subjects and objects by storing the corresponding access rights.

- **Access Control Lists.** Each object has a list of valid subjects with their access rights. This list is called an ACL [14].
- **Capabilities.** Each subject owns a list of objects with corresponding access rights [14].

Also, [14] distinguishes between three different policies:

- **Discretionary Policies.** Discretionary protection regulates subject access to objects based on identities and authorizations that specify the access mode for each subject and each object in the system.
- **Mandatory Policies.** Mandatory policies govern access based on classification of subjects and objects by security level. A security level reflects the sensitivity of the information. The security level of a subject reflects the subject's trustworthiness. The levels are elements of a hierarchically ordered set (e.g. top secret - secret - confidential - unclassified). Depending on the security level of a subject and the object the subject requests, the access is granted or denied.
- **Role-based Policies.** Role-based access controls (RBAC) regulate access based on the activities the user executes in the system. It is required to identify roles which are associated with a set of actions and responsibilities. Access authorization on objects are specified for roles. A user playing a role is allowed to execute all accesses for that role. Roles can be hierarchically organized [14].

  A temporal extension to RBAC is proposed in [6]. Temporal-RBAC adds time-based constraints to the model including periodic role enabling and disabling and temporal dependencies among such actions. A formal description and an implementation is given in [6].

Based on such a policy it is possible to store both allow-rules which give a certain right to a subject (closed system) and deny-rules which explicitly remove a right for a subject (open system) [7]. When both possibilities exist the system has to know in which order the rules should be applied.

Quality of Service. Besides access rights (such as whether or not a subject is allowed to perform a certain action), we also consider with which "quality" an action is executed. Think of applications where customers who want high quality have to pay more than others. Quality can vary along different properties. Related to stream processing, we consider the following.

- **Latency.** How fast will the answer arrive (single tuples).
- **Jitter.** How big are the fluctuations in latency.
- **Bandwidth.** How much data is transferred in a given amount of time.
- **Priority.** Which priority does the user's query have (in relation to others).

4.4   Encryption

To ensure confidentiality of transferred data we have to secure communication links. These links are either inside the system among different nodes in a distributed environment or they are connections from the system to a outside point, e.g. to a client. We have to make sure that only the authorized destination of a data connection is able to read the data. Another issue is data integrity, which ensures that the information is not subject to unauthorized changes during transfer. Both problems can be solved using cryptographic mechanisms such as encryption, electronic signatures and message authentication codes. There are existing protocols such as IPSEC [11] which can be used for that purpose or special protocols could be developed. How such protocols affect QoS when being applied, has to be evaluated.

4.5   Challenges in DSMSs

In contrast to discrete queries (as in database systems) users enter *continuous queries* to process streaming data in DSMSs. As a consequence, the control- and the dataflow is separated (CONTROL CHANNEL and I/O INPUT/OUTPUT CHANNEL).

Further, the QP arranges operators which process data streams and the optimization process *continuously adjusts the query network*. This dynamic reconfiguration has to be considered because data and operations might be merged inside the system and we have to ensure that the results a user gets suit the authorization rules.

Another aspect is the different *user abstraction level* DSMSs provide. Either there is a SQL-like interface (analog to DBMSs) or users work with the system via a box-and-arrow-semantic specifying, a data flow. The security concept has to be implemented according to the used model because the system's changed behavior reflecting the security functionality affects directly the users' interactions with the system.

An important challenge is to keep the impact of the security checks on the *overall system performance* as small as possible (system load, latency, throughput).

5   Security Model

In Sect. 1 we illustrated how an unprotected DSMS can be attacked. We now focus on the problem of *improper release of information* (*data* or *running queries*) and *improper modification* (*outside* or *inside* the system). Based on the general DSMS architecture we propose solutions for these problem classes.

5.1   Secure DSMS Architecture

The three major mechanisms towards a secure DSMS that face the described threats are: First associating an identity with users by authentication, second deciding if and in what way access is allowed by authorization and access control, and third securing communication to ensure confidentiality and integrity.

Figure 2 shows the extended architecture including the security components. One of the design goals was to reduce the impact on the existing system components as much as possible so that every module can still focus on its specific task. The optimization process inside the QP for instance is able to work independently of the security mechanisms. Each of the components, which are described

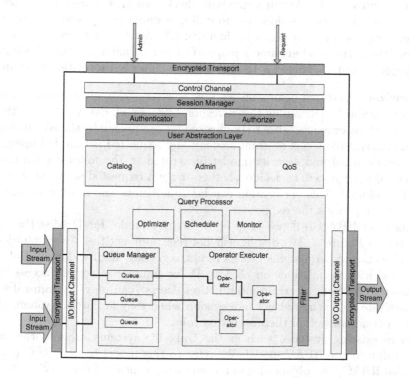

Fig. 2. Secure DSMS Architecture

in the following paragraphs, is responsible for a specific task and can be assigned to one of the described security mechanisms:

a) Associating identities with users and ensuring that to every request for the system the corresponding subject is known
   - SESSION MANAGER
   - AUTHENTICATOR
b) Deciding if, and in what way, access to certain objects is allowed and ensuring that a subject only gets the information it is allowed to see
   - AUTHORIZER
   - USER ABSTRACTION LAYER
   - FILTER
c) Ensuring confidentiality and integrity of transferred requests and data
   - ENCRYPTED TRANSPORT (for input and output streams)
   - ENCRYPTED TRANSPORT (for users' and administrators' requests)

Session Manager. The SESSION MANAGER. assigns each request to a session which belongs to a subject. This assignment is the basis for further authentication and authorization. Before the first request is accepted by the system the user has to prove his identity via the AUTHENTICATOR.

Authenticator. The AUTHENTICATOR checks whether a user is the one he claims to be. This can be done by providing a name and password. There are different ways a user can prove his identity [7]. We do not focus on these any further. The authenticated name is mapped to an internal user-id which identifies the subject uniquely. This id is the basis for the later authorization mechanism.

Authorizer. As stated before, once a user is successfully authenticated, a user-session is established including the corresponding user-id. Every further action or command the user requests has to be checked for permission by the AUTHORIZER.

The AUTHORIZER has to grant or deny any requested action. It implements the access control and security model illustrated in the following paragraph. This enables the system to decide whether or not a requested action on a certain object is allowed. This verification can be done before any other component is instructed to process the request.

Based on RBAC [14], we propose a security model for DSMSs that is illustrated in Figure 3. We distinguish between four entities: Users (subjects), roles, objects and permissions (access rights, e.g. read, modify, delete). Roles are associated with permissions on objects. Roles summarize certain access rights necessary to perform a certain job function. Users "can play" certain roles and they activate one or more roles in a session when they log in the system. Users get the permissions of all their activated roles.

As in existing systems, such as the Unix file systems, we add the owner relationship to the RBAC model. We refer to this model as $OxRBAC$ (owner-extended RBAC). An object always has an owner which is a user. By creating an object (e.g. by inserting a query the instantiated query operators are created)

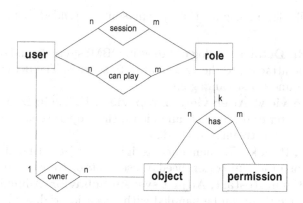

Fig. 3. OxRBAC Security Model

the user becomes the owner of this object and gets all available access rights for it. As a basic set of objects to manage, we propose the following: schema, stream, query, operator, view, and system.

There are several permissions and roles which can be predefined, e.g. an administrator role which has all permissions for controlling the system and changing its behavior, including altering permissions and adding other users and roles.

Furthermore we define the following rule for maximizing security: Everything which is not allowed explicitly is denied, meaning rights have to be assigned explicitly to roles by using allow-rules (closed system).

In contrast to DBMSs, where updates and insertions of data in stored relations are possible, we do not have to consider these actions in a pure data stream environment because the calculated tuples are only read by the clients. Since we believe that an extension to the general architecture will be that DSMSs are able to store data temporally or persistently, we include the corresponding access rights in the following considerations.

We distinguish between three categories of access rights: Rights for users, administrators, and rights relating to connected data sources:

a) User rights:
   - **Read.** The data on an available stream (or on a view of it) can be read. That includes that the user sees the stream and its meta data when he is browsing through the catalog to define his query.
   - **Execute.** Execution refers to operators. By having the right to a certain operator, the user can include it in his query (e.g. a join or an aggregate function).
   - **Insert.** Data can be saved persistently to an attached storage.
   - **Delete.** Stored data can be deleted.
   - **Pass right.** Access rights can be passed to other subjects.
   - **Special operators.** Which operators a user is allowed to perform, e.g. a certain user is only allowed to use an aggregation operator but no join operator.

b) Additionally for managing the system some extended access rights must exist:

- **Attach, Detach.** Analog to tables in DBMSs (create and drop), streams must be attached to the system as data sources. The detach right allows to disconnect a stream again.
- **Create view, Alter view, Drop view.** Unlike in DBMSs where you create, alter or drop tables and views, these operations are only possible on views (on streams) in DSMSs.
- **Grant, Revoke.** To change access rights on objects, the subject (either an owner or an administrator) needs these rights on the corresponding object.
- **Shutdown, Restart, Adjust system behavior.** Administrative operations like these can be handled with execution rights on corresponding functions (which are also modeled as system objects) in the system.

c) Lastly, we manage rights related to data sources. In contrast to DBMSs where users "produce" data in order to store it, in a DSMS information is delivered by the streaming sources. An application which sends data to the system runs on behalf of a certain user. Based on the user's roles (e.g. "information provider"), permissions are managed on that stream object. In this way, information providers are authenticated and only trusted partners are able to send data to the system. To be able to limit the actions an information provider could initiate through sending replacement or deletion tuples as described in [1], we introduce the following rights:

- **Insert.** Normally data is inserted to source streams. Therefore the insert right is needed. Without that right on a certain stream, an information provider cannot interact with the DSMS.
- **Update.** Some providers might send correction messages for previously transferred tuples. For sending such replacement tuples the update right is needed.
- **Delete.** A special case of replacement tuples is a deletion tuple. To be able to delete a previously transmitted tuple, the delete right is necessary.

User Abstraction Layer. To ensure that a subject only gets to see the objects it has permissions for, we provide individual views on the system. Such a view, which only includes objects and operations the subject is allowed to access, is provided by the USER ABSTRACTION LAYER. Considering the use cases of Sect. 1, a user browsing the catalog or looking at running queries only sees the objects he is authorized for. The USER ABSTRACTION LAYER has to establish a relation between the individual views of different subjects and the real internal state of the system, e.g. the whole query network. This component communicates with the AUTHORIZER to check access permissions on objects.

The available interface to interact with a DSMS might be either a descriptive language (analogous to SQL, like CQL [4]) or a formal description of the desired data flow, from source to destination, including the transforming operators in between (like the boxes and arrows in [2]). The USER ABSTRACTION LAYER has to provide a user-specific view on the system corresponding to the used model.

Filter. The second module we introduce to avoid improper release of information is the FILTER at the end of the QP. It ensures that an output stream for a certain subject only contains data the subject is allowed to get. This is necessary because as a result of query optimization it might be possible that streams and operators of different users get combined and merged inside the QP. However, the output of the QP has to be a set of distinguished user streams. By introducing the FILTER we allow the QP and OPTIMIZER to work independently of the security checks. Not only is the implementation easier because every component provides separated services, but the impact on performance will also be smaller as we do not influence any optimization algorithm or constrain the QP in any way. Further, access to output streams of the FILTER has to be synchronized with the corresponding request that produced the output. The request is checked for permission by the USER ABSTRACTION LAYER via the AUTHORIZER. Subsequently the FILTER has to ensure that only an allowed subject gets the corresponding query results. In that way the CONTROL CHANNEL is secured by authorization and the actual data transfer is protected by access control.

Encrypted Transport. We propose to install components in the DSMS architecture to secure data transfers, both at the stream (input and output) and the request side of the system (ENCRYPTED TRANSPORT).

To ensure that data is transferred confidentially so that only the authorized participants are able to access it, we need to encrypt the data and the control channels. Referring to the secured architecture, different levels of encrypting the data transfer are possible.

- **Inside the system.** The flow of information inside the system should be encrypted, especially when we assume that the query processing takes place on different nodes connected via a network.
- **Outside the system.** Both the transferred data via I/O INPUT CHANNEL and I/O OUTPUT CHANNEL and the requests for the system via CONTROL CHANNEL should be secured.

We assume that nodes of the same DSMS can be trusted and the network is under our own control. Then, the second case is the important one because the information leaves the system boundaries and we cannot be sure which path it takes to reach the client.

However, since the purpose of this paper is to develop a security framework for DSMSs, rather than showing how to adopt existing encryption algorithms, details for securing the data transfer are not considered here.

5.2   Example

Considering the use cases illustrated in Sect. 1, the behavior of the DSMS changes with the introduced security mechanisms in following way:

A user connects from a client to the DSMS server by using an encrypted transportation protocol. The server proves its identity by providing a certificate.

After the establishment of that connection through the ENCRYPTED TRANS-PORT the user interacts with the DSMS. Every request which reaches the system through the CONTROL CHANNEL is associated with a session (inside the SESSION MANAGER), which is owned by a certain user. Before being able to perfom any action, the user has to log in, proving his identity. After a successful authenti-cation process inside the AUTHENTICATOR, certain roles the user is allowed to play are activated, a new session is established, and every further request is con-nected to that session. Every action requested by the user can now be checked for permission by the AUTHORIZER. The user browses the catalog, where he only sees objects he is allowed to access through the USER ABSTRACTION LAYER. He inserts a query by using available data sources. The system integrates the inserted query in the internal query network and calculates the results. The user connects to the produced output stream, which is available at the FILTER, by using another encrypted communication link to the ENCRYPTED TRANSPORT at the output side of the DSMS. As the user gets his individual view of the system, he can look at his running queries and modify them. Finally the user logs out and closes the connections to the system.

5.3   Future Issues

For sake of completeness, we briefly want to mention two aspects, that we will not further investigate because of limited space. These are secure distribution and quality of service.

Distribution. Many existing DSMSs, like Borealis [1], include distribution func-tionality for load balancing and high availability. A distributed security concept has to provide solutions for:

- **Trusted authentication.** We have to ensure that a user logged in at one site can use the complete distributed system as one service. Either there is a single point of entry for a user to connect to the whole system, or users can interact with the distributed nodes at different sites.
- **Permission management.** The rules necessary for checking permissions have to be replicated among the participating sites so that access control is possible wherever resources are used.
- **Different administrative domains.** In federated DSMSs, like Medusa [5], sites can be under the control of different administrative domains. Data that is distributed has to be protected from unauthorized access by users working at another site. The access control mechanisms have to work in a global way, prohibiting unwanted disclosure of information. We propose further to introduce the possibility for the users to decide whether or not data processing could be pushed to other sites.
- **Secure communication.** In a distributed environment the secure com-munication inside the system, as mentioned before, becomes important to ensure that only allowed processes connect to output streams of other nodes. The network connecting the sites might be untrusted.

QoS. To provide a QoS-based security service as described in Sect. 4, the QoS module of the system has to be extended too. Depending on the rules defining QoS-properties for subjects, actions must be taken to guarantee them. For instance a subject might be allowed to set the priority of his query to a certain level while others are not allowed to do so.

6 Conclusion

As the adversary scenarios show there are different threats to unprotected DSMSs. In this paper we proposed solutions towards a secure system. We gave a general overview and showed which problems have to be investigated. We focused on two main threat categories: Improper release and improper modification of data. We described the concepts which are necessary to solve these problems. Based on the introduced system architecture we illustrated how the security mechanisms can be implemented. The third problem, denial of service attacks, was partly solved by the authorization process as we did not consider auditing and QoS-related security features in our solution.

The concept we propose in this paper is generic enough to be integrated into any existing data stream management system and therefore an ideal basis for enterprise architectures.

Currently, we are building a first prototype by implementing the proposed security features into Borealis [1], proving that a DSMS can be secured without creating too much of a performance overhead.

References

1. D. J. Abadi, Y. Ahmad, M. Balazinska, U. Cetintemel, M. Cherniack, J.-H. Hwang, W. Lindner, A. S. Maskey, A. Rasin, E. Ryvkina, N. Tatbul, Y. Xing, and S. Zdonik. The Design of the Borealis Stream Processing Engine. In *CIDR*, 2005.
2. D. J. Abadi, D. Carney, U. Çetintemel, M. Cherniack, C. Convey, S. Lee, M. Stonebraker, N. Tatbul, and S. Zdonik. Aurora: A new model and architecture for data stream management. *VLDB Journal*, 2003.
3. D. J. Abadi, W. Lindner, S. Madden, and J. Schuler. An integration framework for sensor networks and data stream management systems. In *VLDB*, 2004.
4. A. Arasu, B. Babcock, S. Babu, M. Datar, K. Ito, R. Motwani, I. Nishizawa, U. Srivastava, D. Thomas, R. Varma, and J. Widom. Stream: The stanford stream data manager. *IEEE Data Engineering Bulletin*, 26(1), 2003.
5. M. Balazinska, H. Balakrishnan, and M. Stonebraker. Contract-based load management in federated distributed systems. In *NSDI*, 2004.
6. E. Bertino, P. A. Bonatti, and E. Ferrari. Trbac: A temporal role-based access control model. *ACM TOISS*, 4(3), 2001.
7. S. Castano, M. Fugini, G. Martella, and P. Samarati. *Database Security*. Addison Wesley, 1994.
8. S. Chandrasekaran, O. Cooper, A. Deshpande, M. Franklin, J. Hellerstein, W. Hong, S. Krishnamurthy, S. Madden, V. Raman, F. Reiss, and M. Shah. TelegraphCQ: Continuous Dataflow Processing for an Uncertain World. In *CIDR*, 2003.

9. M. Cherniack, H. Balakrishnan, M. Balazinska, D. Carney, U. Çetintemel, Y. Xing, and S. Zdonik. Scalable distributed stream processing. In *CIDR*, 2003.
10. J.-H. Hwang, M. Balazinska, A. Rasin, U. Cetintemel, M. Stonebraker, and S. Zdonik. High-Availability Algorithms for Distributed Stream Processing. In *ICDE*, 2005.
11. IETF. IPSec. http://www.ietf.org/html.charters/ipsec-charter.html.
12. J. Krämer and B. Seeger. Pipes - a public infrastructure for processing and exploring streams. In *SIGMOD*, 2004.
13. R. Ramakrishnan and J. Gehrke. *Database Management Systems*, chapter Security and Authorization. Mc Graw Hill, 3rd edition, 2003.
14. Ravi S. Sandhu and Pierrangela Samarati. Access Control: Principles and Practice. *IEEE Communications Magazine*, 32(9), 1994.
15. V. L. Voydock and S. T. Kent. Security mechanisms in high-level network protocols. *ACM Computing Surveys*, 15(2), 1983.
16. S. Zdonik, M. Stonebraker, M. Cherniack, U. Çetintemel, M. Balazinska, and H. Balakrishnan. The Aurora and Medusa Projects. *IEEE Data Engineering Bulletin*, 26(1), 2003.

An Efficient Zoning Technique for Multi-dimensional Access Methods

Byunggu Yu[1] and Seon Ho Kim[2]

[1] Computer Science Department, University of Wyoming,
Laramie, WY 82071, USA
yu@uwyo.edu
[2] Computer Science Department, University of Denver,
Denver, CO 80208, USA
seonkim@cs.du.edu

Abstract. In emerging database applications that deal with large sets of multi-dimensional data, the performance of the query system significantly depends on the performance of its access methods and the underlying disk system. In recent years, hard disks are manufactured with multiple physical zones, where seek times and data transfer rates vary significantly across the zones. However, there is a marked lack of investigation on how to optimize multidimensional access methods given a zoned disk model. The paper proposes a novel *dynamic* zoning technique called *DMD-Zoning* that can be applied to a variety of multidimensional access methods and that can fully utilize zoning characteristics of hard disks for busy multi-user database systems.

1 Introduction

In recent years, hard disks are manufactured with *zoned recording* (or *zoning*), which groups adjacent disk cylinders into zones [10,17]. Tracks are longer towards the outer portions of a disk platter as compared to the inner portions. Hence, more data can be recorded in the outer tracks when the maximum linear density, i.e., bits per inch, is applied to all tracks. The results are multiple physical zones in a disk, where seek times and data transfer rates vary significantly across the zones. However, there is a marked lack of investigation on how to optimize dynamic multidimensional access methods (i.e., multidimensional access methods that can efficiently accommodate insert and delete operations at run-time without reorganizing the entire index structure) given a zoned disk model. Instead, conventional access methods have been developed based on a traditional disk model that comes with many simplifying assumptions such as an average seek-time and a single data transfer rate.

The performance of an access method of database can be improved when the following conditions are met: *Cond.* 1. The index structure of the access method is split into disjoint parts each of which is stored in a specific disk zone in its entirety; *Cond.* 2. At every point in time, all running threads are accessing only one zone and a thread accesses another zone only after it completes all required accesses to the current zone.

Because the physical zones of a disk do not necessarily have the same data transfer rate, we can further optimize the performance by modifying Cond. 1 as follows:

D. Draheim and G. Weber (Eds.): TEAA 2005, LNCS 3888, pp. 129–143, 2006.

Modified Cond. 1: more frequently accessed pages are stored in a faster zone. Considering a tree-type index structure and random queries, one can think of approximating the access frequency of each page by means of the level of the page in the index structure. For example, the root page of an index structure has the highest access frequency among the pages constituting the index structure, since every search must access the root. In this sense, the leaf level pages are associated with the lowest access frequency. Therefore, the level of a page in the index structure determines the zone in which the page is stored. This is a simple and straightforward approach that can be applied to any tree-type index structure and the basis of the idea of pinning a few top levels of an active index structure in the database buffer space [7]. However, this approach ignores the underlying data distribution, and all queries that produce a non-empty result must access all the zones. In fact, this approach is based on the assumption that all pages at the same level are equally important and have the same likelihood of being accessed by a random query. In practice, this is not the case.

For each unknown random range query, a page that has a larger range in the data space is more likely accessed. Considering non-uniformly distributed data objects, it is often the case with any index structure that a page has a larger range in the data space than an upper level page that is not a direct ancestor. In addition, when the query distribution follows the underlying data distribution, a page that encloses more data objects in the data space has a higher access probability. Moreover, in many applications, the queries have no "affinity" for certain dimensions or the query patterns often change over time. In this case, all dimensions are equally important, and a page that has a smaller perimeter in the data space tends to have a lower average access frequency. Therefore, the access frequency of each page should be determined by the actual region of the page in the data space and, optionally, the number of data objects that the page encloses. Consequently, the placement of a page on to a specific disk zone is determined by its access frequency.

To meet Cond. 2, one can consider locking-based approach. While a specific zone is being accessed by one or more threads, all the other zones on the same disk must be locked. The locking-based approach incurs additional waiting time that is more pronounced when a thread is allowed to access another zone before it completes all necessary accesses to the current zone, since the search thread should wait for the zone to be unlocked each time it moves into a different zone. Therefore, an efficient search thread control mechanism needs to be developed.

This paper proposes a novel dynamic zoning technique called the *DMD-Zoning* (*Dynamic Multi-Dimensional Zoning*) that can be applied to a variety of one- or multi-dimensional access methods and that can fully utilize zoning characteristics of hard disks. In the *DMD-Zoning*, index structures are placed in such a way that all disk zones are almost equally utilized and that more frequently accessed index pages are stored in a faster disk zone (this meets Modified Cond. 1). Then the generalized query processing technique of the *DMD-Zoning* significantly improves the query performance by reducing page retrieval times from the hard disk (this meets Cond. 2). For a focused discussion, this paper considers only a single disk case. However, the techniques proposed in this paper can be generalized to multi-disk (e.g., RAID) systems.

2 Multi-zone Disks

One of the most important physical characteristics of a modern magnetic disk drive is its zones: a disk consists of several zones, each providing a different storage capacity and transfer rate. *Zoned recording* (or *zoning*) is an approach utilized by disk manufactures to increase the storage capacity of various types of disks [10]. This technique groups adjacent disk cylinders into zones [10,17]. Tracks are longer towards the outer portions of a disk platter as compared to the inner portions; hence, more data may be recorded in the outer tracks when the same maximum linear density (i.e., bits per inch) is applied to all tracks. A zone is a contiguous collection of disk cylinders whose tracks have the same storage capacity, i.e., the number of sectors per track is constant in the same zone. Hence, outer zones have more sectors per track than inner zones. Different disk models have different number of zones (e.g., Seagate Cheetah X15 has 9 zones; Seagate Barracuda 7200.7 has 15 zones). Different zones provide different transfer rates because: 1) the storage capacity of the tracks for each zone is different, and 2) the disk platters rotate at a fixed number of revolutions per second.

A multi-zone disk consists of multiple disk zones. Each disk zone consists of one or more disk cylinders. Note that all cylinders in the same zone have the same data transfer rate. A rotational latency is determined by the disk revolution time. A seek time between two locations on a disk, x cylinders apart, can be calculated using a practical non-linear approximation, $seek(x)$ [17]. A *page read/write time* consists of a seek time, a rotational latency, and a page transfer time.

3 Zoned Index Structure

In most secondary storage access methods, the index structure is a hierarchy of index pages that form a balanced tree with a single root. At every level of the structure, the d-dimensional data space is recursively divided into *hyper-rectangles*. The rectangle of the *root page* encloses the entire data set.

The *leaf pages* contain the actual data objects or *data entries*. A *data entry <coordinates, tuple_pointer>* contains the location (*coordinates*) of a d-dimensional point data in the space and the address (*tuple_pointer*) of the corresponding data record (object) in the underlying database. Every *interior page* contains *index entries*. An *index entry* is a *<region_descriptor, child_pointer>* pair, where *region_descriptor* represents the minimum hyper-rectangle enclosing all the data points stored in the leaf pages of the subtree rooted at the child page indicated by the *child_pointer*. In spatial access methods (SAMs) that are designed for regional data objects, coordinates of every data entry is replaced by *region_descriptor* of the corresponding regional data object[1]. Thus, SAMs can be easily modified to index point data.

An index structure is built and updated in two ways: 1) bulk-updating and 2) dynamic updates. In the latter case, each data object is inserted or deleted at run-time.

---

[1] Typical approximations of regions in space include minimum bounding rectangles (MBRs), minimum bounding circles (MBCs), and minimum bounding polygons (MBPs). Since MBR-based approximations are characterized by intermediate complexity and accuracy, they tend to be used more frequently [1,6,7,8,11,12,13].

An efficient dynamic update algorithm for an index structure is required when the index structure is used in an operational database in a transactional environment.

In recent years, efficient bulk-updating algorithms are required in many database applications where static index structures are built on a populated data set that is seldom or periodically updated. For example, in many databases for analytical tasks (e.g., data warehouses and data marts), index structures are built on an already populated data set. Each update (if there is) typically inserts or deletes a relatively large number of data objects. Bulk-updating is based on a bulk-loading or packing algorithm that can build or reorganize an index structure on an existing data set. A bulk-loading algorithm is typically designed for a certain index structure. For example, a bulk-loading algorithm for B-trees and a bulk-loading algorithm for R-trees can be found in [15] and [5,8,16], respectively. In general, bulk-loading algorithms produce a rather optimized index structure due to the fact that bulk-loading algorithms start with a whole data set. However, to the best of our knowledge, no investigation has been done on how to optimize access methods given a multi-zone disk model.

To avoid any possible confusions and misunderstanding, we first define the following measures: *Definition* 1. The *area* of an index page that is associated with a d-dimensional hyper-rectangle R in the data space is defined as $\prod_{i=1}^{d}(h_i - l_i)$ where, for all $i=1,\ldots,d$, h_i and l_i are the high- and low-endpoints of R along dimension i; *Definition* 2. The *margin* of an index page that is associated with a d-dimensional hyper-rectangle R in the data space is defined as $2 \cdot \sum_{i=1}^{d}(h_i - l_i)$ where, for all $i=1,\ldots,d$, h_i and l_i are the high- and low-endpoints of R along dimension i.

3.1 Static Zoning of Index Structure

Given a complete static index structure (i.e., index structures that are built and updated by a bulk-updating algorithm), our static zoning algorithm distributes the index pages among multiple zones. First, let us define two functions: *Measure(p)* is a function that returns either area or margin of a page p; *Pop(p)* is a function that returns the number of objects contained by the leaf level of the subtree rooted at p (i.e., the number of the data objects within the region of p). As discussed in Sect. 1, the zone in which p is stored should be determined by *Measure(p)* and *Pop(p)*. Now, let *MeasureU* and *PopU* be the area (or margin) of the root page and the total number of the data objects, respectively. Then one can consider the following weighted sum as an estimated access probability of a page p for an unknown query:

$$E(p) = W1 \times \frac{Measure(p)}{MeasureU} + W2 \times \frac{Pop(p)}{PopU}, \tag{1}$$

where $0 \leq W1 \leq 1$, $0 \leq W2 \leq 1$, and $W1 + W2 = 1$.

Considering a large database, the estimated access probability of a leaf page can be very small (i.e., close to zero). The root page is always accessed (i.e., the access probability is 1). If the distribution of the queries does not follow the distribution of the data, $W1=1$ and $W2=0$. We assume this through the rest of this paper.

Now, let NZ and Cap be the number of the zones (i.e., the number of available zones, or a set of selected zones that are under-filled or dedicated to index structures) and the total sum of the zone capacities, respectively. We sequentially number the given (selected) zones in such a way that a smaller zone number (*zid*) is always associated with a faster zone (in terms of page read/write time). In addition, let us use *ZCap*[*zid*] to denote the storage capacity of zone *zid*.

Given a static index structure, our simple static zoning algorithm sorts all pages of the index structure in descending order by their E value (i.e., Eq. 1). Then, from the first page with the highest E value, the algorithm assigns $ZR[zid] \times TS$ pages to each given zone *zid*, where TS is the total number of pages constituting the index structure and $ZR[zid] = ZCap[zid] / Cap$, for all *zid*=0,..,*NZ*-1. Note that *zid* 0 represents the fastest zone among the given *NZ* zones. This can evenly distribute the index pages across all selected disk zones, resulting in a uniform utilization of the zone spaces.

3.2 Dynamic Zoning of Index Structure

Dynamic zoning of an index structure is required when the data set is frequently updated. Dynamic zoning is much more challenging than the above mentioned static zoning because, when an index page is modified at run-time by an insert or delete operation, the zone in which the modified page is stored must be decided solely based on the local information. Thus, without careful consideration, index pages could be placed in a skewed way, which may cause skewed zone usages.

Our novel approach is to assign index pages to the zones in such a way that all given zones are utilized as equally as possible. Given an index tree that has TS pages and NZ disk zones, we define disk *zone utilization indicator* (*ZUI*) as follows:

$$ZUI[i] = ZC[i]/(TS \times ZR[i]), \; i = 0,..., (NZ - 1), \tag{2}$$

where $ZC[i]$ is the actual number of index pages that are stored in zone i, and $(TS \times ZR[i])$ is the number of index pages that are stored in zone i when the zones are equally utilized. Note that $ZUI[i] > 1$ represents that zone i is over-utilized (i.e., too many index pages in the zone) while $ZUI[i] < 1$ means that zone i is under-utilized.

Now, let *Measure*(*p*), *MinM*, and *MaxM* be the area (or margin) of an index page *p*, the minimum recorded value of *Measure*, and the maximum recorded value of *Meaure* (note that $MaxM = Measure(root)$) in the given index tree, respectively. Then, we define the *Relative Importance* (*RI*) of *p* as follows:

$$RI(p) = \begin{cases} \dfrac{Measure(p) - MinM}{MaxM - MinM} & \text{if } MaxM \neq MinM, \\ 1 & \text{otherwise.} \end{cases} \tag{3}$$

Equation 3 assumes that the queries are random and do not follow the distribution of data. Note that we can modify Eq. 3 as shown in Eq. 1 when the distribution of the queries follows the distribution of the data. The dynamic zoning algorithm (Fig. 1) of the *DMD-Zoning* assigns each index page to a specific zone based on Eqs. 2 and 3.

Please observe that the *for-loop* (A) in Fig. 1 considers the zones in a descending order by *zid*. We do this because of the following characteristics of tree-type index structures: (1) The area and margin of index pages rapidly decrease downward the tree; (2) The number of index pages increases at an exponential rate downward the

```
int Dynamic_Zoning(index_page)
{
    double C_ZR; //Cumulative ratio of the following measure:
    double Measure;

    Measure = Volume(index_page); // or Margin(index_page);

    //Update MinMeasure and MaxMeasure
    if(Measure < MinMeasure) MinMeasure = Measure;
    if(Measure > MaxMeasure) MaxMeasure = Measure;

    //Define relative importance (RI) of index_page
    if(MinMeasure == MaxMeasure) RI = 1.0;
    else RI=(Measure-MinMeasure)/(MaxMeasure-MinMeasure);

    //Assign a zone to an index page
    for(C_ZR=0, i=0; i<NZ; i++) { //-----------------------------------------(A)
            ZUI = ZC[NZ-i-1]/ (TS*ZR[NZ-i-1]);
            C_ZR += ZR[NZ-i-1];
            if(RI <= C_ZR && ZUI <= 1)
                    return(NZ-i-1);
    }
    return(0);
}
```

Fig. 1. Dynamic Zoning

tree. Combined, these characteristics of tree-type index structures result in the following: most index pages have a very low RI value. Through our experiments, we found that when the ZUI condition is not considered in (A), most index pages are stored in the last (slowest) one or two zones and that, in many cases, only the root page is stored in the first (fastest) zone. This skewed usage of zones aggravates the query performance and leaves many zones under utilized. In our zoning algorithm (Fig. 1), those pages stacked in the slowest zones are shifted towards the fastest (first) zone in such a way that all given zones are utilized as equally as possible (the experimental evidences will be presented in Sect. 5).

4   Query Processing

A range query with a region initiates a selection process that starts with the root page and propagates downward, traversing potentially multiple paths in the tree. At each interior page, the entries are tested to select the child pages that satisfy the search predicate. In general, the search predicate tests whether the region of the child page intersect with the *minimum bounding rectangle (MBR)* of the given query region. Whenever a leaf page is accessed, the procedure selects all resident objects or data entries that fall within the query region. The point query is a special case of range query, where the query range is infinitesimally small. SAMs provide several different types of range queries (topological queries) and the query processing procedure is more complicated. An in-depth coverage of this is found in [12,13].

```
NZ // the total number of existing zones (an environmental constant)
zone_locks[NZ] // an integer semaphore array; one for each zone
ZR[NZ] // ZR[i] is the ratio (the capacity of zone i)/(the disk capacity)
struct index_queue {
          PID; //a page ID
          Level; //an index tree level
}
index_queue IPA[NZ][ ];   // each zone is associated with a FIFO
                          // queue of the IDs of the pages to be accessed
                          // by currently running threads.
// all disk page I/Os come through the following three wrappers:
read_page (PID) { // PID is a page ID
    if PID is in the buffer then access the page in the buffer
    else {
          wait (zone_locks[zone(PID)]); //a semaphore operation
          //e.g., semop() Linux/Unix call with sem_num=zone(PID)
          //and sem_op = -1;
          //zone(PID) returns the current zone ID of the PID.
          read the page PID from the disk;
          signal (zone_locks[zone(PID)]);
          //e.g., semop() Linux/Unix call with sem_num=zone(PID)
          //and sem_op = 1;
    }
}
write_page_on_disk (page, zid) {
          wait (zone_locks[zid]); //a semaphore operation
          write page on the disk;
          signal (zone_locks[zid]); //a semaphore operation
}
write_index_page_on_disk (index_page, old_zid) {
    int new_zid;
    new_zid = Dynamic_Zoning (index_page);
    if (old_zid != null) { // index_page is on the disk
          TS = 1; ZC[old_zid] -= 1; // the page is removed
    }
    TS += 1; ZC[new_zid] += 1; //placed in zone new_zoneID
    write_page_on_disk (index_page, new_zid);
}
```

Fig. 2. The system-wide components of the DMD-Zoning

An index search involves a sequence of page accesses. In order to take complete advantage of a zoned index structure, each index search must be localized. That is, each search must be a sequence of zone-bursts, where a zone-burst is a sequence of all necessary page accesses to a certain zone. This is because of the fact that accessing two pages located in two different zones is slower than accessing two pages in the same zone due to an increased seek time. Thus, the number of moves across the disk zones must be minimized. However, in a given tree, an index page p can possibly have a higher RI than a higher level page p' has if p' is not an ancestor of p. Moreover, pages at the same level can have different RIs. Therefore, neither depth-first nor breadth-first implementation of the search procedure can guarantee this localized search.

Although different index pages can have different RI values, the dynamic zoning algorithm of the *DMD-Zoning* guarantees that an index page always has a lower RI

```
TS; //the total no. of index pages constituting the index tree
ZC[NZ]; //ZC[i] is the no. of index pages stored in zone i

search_main (q) //q is a range query
{
    current_depth = 1; //the root level is level 1
    read_page(root);
    if(current_depth==tree_height) { //root is the only leaf page
        get_result(D);
    }
    else {
        for(i=0; i<NZ; i++) wait(zone_locks[i]); //lock all zones
        first_zone = NZ;
        for each index entry I_i {
            if check_predicate(I_i) {
                if(zone(I_i.child_pointer) < first_zone)
                    first_zone = zone(I_i.child_pointer);
                add_queue(I_i);
            }
        }
        for (i=first_zone, i<NZ; i++) { ---------------------- (B)
            signal(zone_locks[i]); //unlock zone i
            zone_search(i);
            wait (zone_locks[i]); //lock zone i
        }
        // The query has been completed;
        for(i=0; i<NZ; i++)
            signal(i); //release all zone
    }
}
```

```
zone_search (zid)
{
    int pid, level;
    while(IPA[zid] queue is not empty) repeat {
        <pid, level> = get_fifo(IPA[zid]);
        read_page(pid);
        if(level == tree_height) { // pid is a leaf
            get_result(D);
        }
        else {
            for each index entry I_i {
                if check_predicate(I_i)
                    add_queue(I_i);
            }
        }
    } //while loop
}
get_result (D) {
    for each data entry D_i {
        if D_i satisfies the query predicate
            add D_i to the result set.
    }
}
add_queue (I_i) {
    add <I_i.child_pointer, current_depth+1>
        to IPA[zone(I_i.child_pointer)] queue;
}
```

Fig. 3. The generalized query processing algorithm of the DMD-Zoning

value (i.e., a smaller area and margin) than all of its ancestors at a higher level. That is, along each search path downward the tree, the involved zones are always in an ascending order by *zid*. Note that to guarantee that this condition always holds, every modified page is written on the disk by the function *write_index_page_on_disk()* in Fig. 2. In addition, the zone of every ancestor page of the modified page must be recalculated by the same function upward the tree in a single atomic transaction. Under this condition, the generalized search algorithm (Figs. 2 and 3) of the *DMD-Zoning* can ensure that each search is a sequence of *zone-bursts* and each involved zone is associated with only one of the bursts of the search. Furthermore, since the algorithm is generalized, it can be applied to a vast majority of tree-type access methods. Note that, in Fig. 3, each *zone_search()* call in the *for-loop* (B) represents a single zone-burst and that the FIFO queue array *IPA* in Fig. 2 is updated by the functions in Fig. 3.

5   Experimental Results

In order to validate that the proposed *DMD-Zoning* can significantly improve the performance of access methods, we performed a set of experiments with the original R*-tree (with 30% forced-reinsertion at the leaf level) [1] and two versions of DMD-Zoned R*-trees called the *Area-Zoned R*-tree* and the *Margin-Zoned R*-tree*.

In the original R*-tree, index pages are placed on a disk without any consideration of physical zones. While the Area-Zoned R*-tree used the area in calculating the *RI* (Equation 3) of each individual index page, the *RI* of each page of the Margin-Zoned R*-tree was calculated based on its margin in the data space. The *DMD-Zoning* was actually implemented in both the Area-Zoned R*-tree and the Margin-Zoned R*-tree. In the experiments, a disk model of Seagate Barracuda 7200.7 with 15 zones was used. All the disk zones were used for storing the index structures (i.e., $NZ = 15$). We assumed one-page-buffer and no-pre-fetching to concentrate our focus on disk I/O time[2]. All values (coordinate values and pointer values) stored in the tested structures were 4 bytes long.

In the first experiment with uniformly distributed data, the number of dimensions was varied between 2 and 64. The page size was fixed at 8K (8,192) bytes. For each d-dimensional space $[0,1]^d$, a data file of 131,072 (2^{17}) randomly generated point objects was generated. Data objects (records) of each file were inserted into all three variants of the R*-tree. The retrieval performance of the access methods was measured over four sets of 2,000 range queries. In first three sets, each side of a random query rectangle was obtained by generating a random center and extending it along the dimension parallel to the side by 0.02, 0.1, and 0.25. In the last query set, each query was generated as follows: 1) randomly generate the center point; 2) extend the query along every dimension so that the volume of the query is 0.0001. That is, in the last query set, each unclipped query range covered 0.01% of the data space. In all query sets, the query rectangles that intersect the boundary of the data space were properly clipped.

The results of the experiment given in Fig. 4a show that our zoned R*-trees improve the range query performance by reducing the *average page access time* (average time required for a query to read all necessary index pages from the disk). As shown in the figure, the proposed zoning techniques (i.e., the Area-Zoned R*-tree and Margin-Zoned R*-tree) constantly reduce the average page access time per query compared to that of the R*-tree by 57.8 – 61.2%. That is, the zoned R*-trees were about 2.4 – 2.6 times faster than the original R*-tree in processing the range queries.

To further discuss the effectiveness of the *DMD-Zoning* technique, we considered the *zone utilization indicator* (*ZUI*) defined in Equation 2. Fig. 4b shows the *ZUI*s of both the Area-Zoned R*-tree and the Margin-Zoned R*-tree. Please note that, as defined in Equation 2, a ZUI of 1.0 does not mean that the storage space of the zone is full, but means that a desirable amount of index data (i.e., the denominator in Equation 2) is stored in the zone. In the figure, one can find that all zones are almost equally utilized especially in higher dimensional spaces. In low dimensional spaces, zone 0 is underutilized. To understand the reason for this, one should consider the following properties of tree-type index structures with a fixed page size: (1) As the number of dimensions increases, the size of each individual entry becomes larger because each entry has more coordinate values; (2) As the number of dimensions

---

[2] As a side note: In transactional environments, many transactions and queries are concurrently processed over numerous data sets and indices, and each query is allocated only a small fraction of the database buffer. Many database query optimizers (e.g., the cost-based query optimizer of Oracle8) assume that each query will be executed on a busy multi-user system with a fairly low buffer cache hit rate.

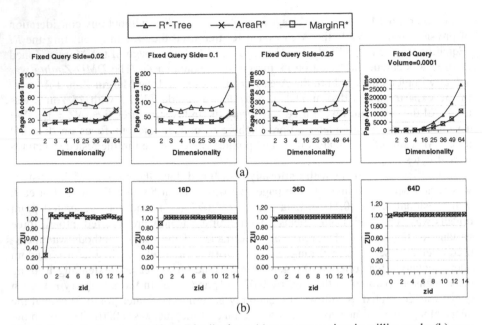

Fig. 4. Synthetic Random Uniform Distributions: (a) page access time in milliseconds; (b) zone utilization indicator (ZUI)

increases, the maximum number of entries that can be stored in a single page decreases because the page size is fixed and the entry size increases.

These mean that the average fanout[3] of a lower dimensional index tree is larger than that of a higher dimensional index tree. In addition, given the same number of data objects, a lower dimensional index tree consists of a smaller number of pages than a higher dimensional index tree does. For example, in the experiment, the 2-dimensional, 16-dimensional, and 64-dimensional R-trees consisted of 280, 1616, and 6550 pages. Therefore, storing one more or one less page in a zone resulted in a larger increase or decrease in the zone utilization (Equation 2) in a lower dimensional case.

Moreover, the measure (i.e., area or margin) decreases downward the tree at a rate that is a function of the fanout. This rate of a lower dimensional structure is much higher than that of a higher dimensional structure, because of the larger fanout of the lower dimensional structure. This results in huge gaps among a few top *RI* (Equation 3) values. For example, in the experiments with two-dimensional data set (i.e., 2D case in Fig. 4b), zone 0 and zone 1 contained 2 and 9 pages, respectively, although both zones have the same capacity. That is, there was only zero (this is possible because of the page shifting of *Dynamic_Zoning* algorithm in Sect. 3.2) or one page that had an *RI* value that was close enough to the root's *RI* to position itself in zone 0.

In the second experiment with synthetic skewed data, each tested data file had 131,072 (2^{17}) randomly generated points focused mainly in ten different clusters. Each cluster was randomly located in the universe and had an extent that varied

---

[3] In a typical index tree that splits each overfilled page into two halves, the average fanout (page utilization) is about $\ln2 \times C$, where C is the maximum number of entries that can be stored in a page [11].

between 0.05 and 0.3 along each dimension. The clusters were populated using 101,072 random data objects. Then 30,000 points were randomly scattered through the entire universe. The query performance was measured using the four query sets used in the first experiment.

The results (Fig. 5) of the experiment with skewed data also demonstrate the same trend as those with uniform data: the proposed *DMD-Zoning* (i.e., the Area-Zoned R*-tree and Margin-Zoned R*-tree) reduces the average page access time of the R*-tree by 57.5-62%. The *ZUI*s of the Area-Zoned R*-tree were similar to those in Fig. 4. However, this time, the Margin-Zoned R*-tree showed a higher *ZUI* on zone 0 when a high-dimensional data set was given. This is what we actually expected – given the same structure, the area of index pages decreases downward the tree at a much faster rate than the margin of index pages does, especially in a higher dimensional space. One can further observe this by comparing Definitions 1 and 2 in Sect. 3.2 with the changing factor d. This resulted in a couple of slightly underutilizes zones in slower, but larger, zones (zones 12, 13, and 14 in Fig. 5b). Consequently, preceding zones had too many pages and sent some pages towards zone 0.

The last experiment was conducted over a large real data set. Our real data set represented a database table of 1,028,872 records. This data table was obtained from a database of a telecommunication company. The original table has 19 attributes of different types. However, by breaking the values of certain attributes and applying simple transformations, we obtained an array of 25-dimensional points with 4-byte unsigned long coordinates (nulls were replaced by a value of zero). Using an order-preserving domain transformation, the values of each attribute were normalized to a range of floating-point numbers between 0 and 1. Then, by multiplying each attribute

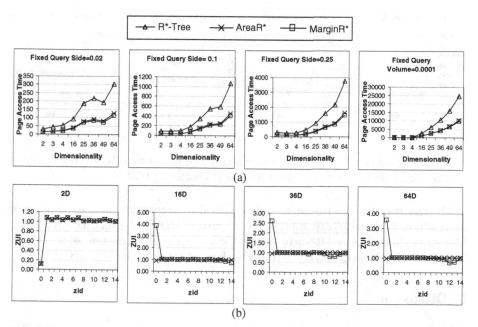

Fig. 5. Synthetic Skewed Distributions: (a) page access time in milliseconds; (b) zone utilization indicator (ZUI)

value by 2^{32} and rounding the result, we obtained the data points in a universe with 25 dimensions, each of which was 4 bytes long. Analyzing this set, we found that exactly 303,278 objects had no null values and that each of the rest of the data objects (i.e., 725,594 records) had about 2.18 nulls on average. The objects having one or more nulls appear on the boundary of the universe. That is, over 70% of the data points were located on the boundary of the universe.

To measure the performance of the R*-tree variants, five sets of range queries were generated. In the first two query sets, the side length (extent) of every query was fixed at 0.1 and 0.25, recursively. As before, the queries that intersect the boundary of the data space were clipped. In the other three sets, query rectangles had a fixed volume of 0.0001, 0.01, and 0.1. Again, some queries were clipped. Every query set had 3,000 queries.

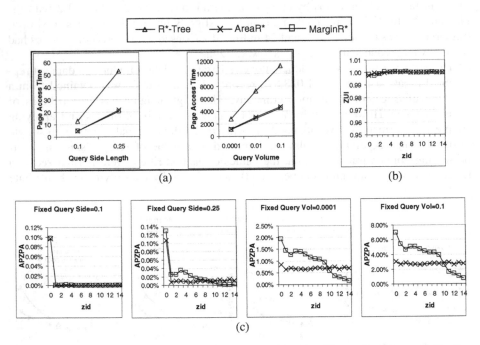

Fig. 6. Large Real Data Distribution: (a) page access time in milliseconds; (b) zone utilization indicator (ZUI); (c) average percentage of zoned pages accessed (APZPA)

The results of the experiment given in Fig. 6 also demonstrate the same trend as in the results of the previous experiments: the proposed *DMD-Zoning* (i.e., the Area-Zoned R*-tree and Margin-Zoned R*-tree) reduces the average page access time of the R*-tree by 58.2-62.1%. Furthermore, Fig. 6 shows the best *ZUIs* that we have observed.

6 Discussion

Table 1 summarizes the experimental results presented and discussed in Sect. 5. The percentage improvements represent $100 \times (RT_{R*} - RT_{DMD}) / RT_{R*}$, where RT_{R*} is the page access time (average time required for a query to read all necessary index pages from the disk) of the original R*-tree and RT_{DMD} is the page access time of the R*-tree improved by the *DMD-Zoning* (Area-Zoned or Margin-Zoned). As shown in the table, the *DMD-Zoning* constantly improved the performance of the R*-tree by about 60% in all tested cases.

To compare the Margin-Zoned R*-tree and the Area-Zoned R*-tree, we considered the following measure: *Average Percentage of Zoned Pages Accessed* by a single query (*APZPA*). Fig. 6c shows the APZPAs of both the Area-Zoned R*-tree and the Margin-Zoned R*-tree tested on the 25-dimensional real data introduced in Sect. 5. As discussed in Sect. 1 (*Modified Condition* 1), when the pages that are stored in a faster zone actually have a higher access frequency (i.e., more pages required by a query are found in faster zones), the query performance is further improved. That is, we want a faster zone to have a higher *APZPA* value.

Table 1. Percentage Improvements

Data Distribution	Margin-Zoned R*-tree	Area-Zoned R*-tree
uniform	58.4 – 61.2%	57.8 – 59.9%
clusters	58.3 – 62%	57.5 – 60%
real	60.1 – 62.1%	58.2 – 61.9%

In Table 1 that summarizes our experimental results, one can find that the improvements of the Margin-Zoned R*-tree are higher than those of the Area-Zoned R*-tree by a small margin. One can find the reason for this by observing Fig. 6c: The Margin-Zoned R*-tree's *APZPAs* are better than those of the Area-Zoned R*-tree. While the Margin-Zoned R*-tree's average page access frequencies are nicely skewed towards the fastest zone, the Area-Zoned R*-tree shows rather flat *APZPAs*. That is, in our experiments, the Margin-Zoned R*-tree was better than the Area-Zoned R*-tree in estimating (i.e., *RI*, Equation 3) the actual access frequencies of the pages. In contrast, although both of the Area-Zoned R*-tree and the Margin-Zoned R*-tree showed excellent (i.e., almost equal) zone utilizations in most cases, the Area-Zoned R*-tree showed a better *ZUIs* in the experiment with the synthetic skewed data (Fig. 5).

In closing this section, we put an emphasis on the fact that the *DMD-Zoning* technique can improve virtually any access method. In the paper, we presented two variants of the *DMD-Zoning* (one is the margin-based zoning and the other is the area-based zoning) that can enhance any access method that employs a hierarchy of pages as the index structure. For example, the presented *DMD-Zoning* can be directly applied to the following access methods without any modifications: *KDB-tree* variants [11,14], *R-tree* variants [1,3,6,13], *QSF-tree* variants [12], and *B-tree* variants [4]. Because rectangular approximations (or grouping) of regions are characterized by intermediate complexity and accuracy, they tend to be used more frequently. However, there are different access methods, such as the SS-tree [18], the TV-tree [9], and the Pyramid technique [2], that employ a different approximation of regions. One can easily apply the DMD-Zoning to any hierarchical access method that employs a non-rectangular approximation or grouping by simply changing the measures in Definitions 1 and 2.

7 Conclusion

In recent years, an increasing number of database applications deal with large sets of static or dynamic multidimensional data. In these applications, the query performance is heavily dependent on the available access methods and the underlying disk system. Unlike traditional disk models, recently developed disk models provide multiple zones in a disk, where seek times and data transfer rates vary significantly across the zones. Although efficient index optimizations, such as bulk-loading and packing algorithms, have been developed for large static data, there is a marked lack of investigation on how to optimize multidimensional access methods given a zoned disk model.

In this paper, we proposed a novel zoned access technique that can significantly enhance the query performance of a wide variety of access methods by taking into account the different page read/write times of the disk zones. The proposed index zoning algorithms can zone virtually any static or dynamic hierarchical (tree-type) index structure in such a way that all disk zone spaces are equally utilized and that more frequently accessed pages are stored in a faster zone. Then the proposed generalized query algorithm makes each search be a sequence of zone-bursts, where each involved zone is associated with only one of the bursts. In the presented experiments, the proposed zoned access technique, called the *DMD-Zoning*, improved the query performance of the R*-tree by an almost constant factor of 2.5.

In our future research, we will consider zoned multi-disk models, concurrency control, and different type queries, such as the k-nearest neighbor query.

References

1. Beckman, N., et. Al., The R*-tree: An Efficient and Robust Access Method for Points and Rectangles. In *ACM SIGMOD International Conference on Management of Data*, pages 322-331, 1990.
2. Berchtold, S., Bohm, C., & Kriegel, H.-P. (1998). The Pyramid-technique: Towards breaking the curse of dimensionality. *Proc. ACM SIGMOD Int. Conf. on Management of Data* (pp. 142-153).
3. Berchtold, S. Keim, D., & Kriegel, H.-P. (1996). The X-tree: An index structure for high-dimensional data. *Proc. VLDB Int. Conf. on Very Large Data Bases* (pp. 28-39).
4. Comer, D., "The Ubiquitous B-tree," *ACM Computing Surveys* 11, pp. 121-137, 1979.
5. Faloutsos, C. and Kamel, I. On Packing R-tree. In *Proceedings of the ACM International Conference on Information and Knowledge Management (CIKM)*, pages 490-499, 1993.
6. Guttman, A. (1984). R-trees: A dynamic index structure for spatial searching. *Proc. ACM SIGMOD Int. Conf. on Management of Data*, pp. 47-54.
7. Leutenegger, S.T. and Lopez, M.A., The Effect of Buffering on the Performance of R-trees. *IEEE Transactions on Knowledge and Data Engineering,* 12(1):33-44, 2000.
8. Leutenegger, S.T. and Lopez, M.A. and Edingnton, J.M., STR: A Simple and Efficient Algorithm for R-tree Packing. *IEEE International Conference on Data Engineering*, pages 497-506, 1997.
9. Lin, K., Jagadish, H., and Faloutsos, C. (1995). The TV-tree: An Index Structure for High-Dimensional Data. *VLDB Journal.* Vol. 3, pp. 517-542.
10. Ng, S.W., Advances in Disk Technology: Performance Issues. *IEEE Computer Magazine*, pages 75-81, 1998.

11. Orlandic, R., & Yu, B. (2002). A Retrieval Technique for High-Dimensional Data and Partially Specified Queries. *DKE Data & Knowledge Engineering, Elsevier* 42(2), pp. 1-21.
12. Orlandic, R. and Yu, B., Scalable QSF-Trees: Retrieving Regional Objects in High-Dimensional Spaces, Journal of *Database Management, Idea Group Publishing,* 15(3): 45-59, 2004.
13. Papadias, D. Theodoridis, Y., Sellis, T., & Egenhofer, M.J. (1995). Topological relations in the world of minimum bounding rectangles: A study with R-trees. *Proc. ACM SIGMOD Int. Conf. on Management of Data* (pp. 92-103).
14. Robinson, J.T. (1981). The K-D-B Tree: A Search Structure for Large Multidimensional Dynamic Indexes. *Proc. ACM SIGMOD Int. Conf. on Management of Data* (pp. 10-18).
15. Rosenberg, A.L. and Snyder, L., Time- and Space- Optimality in B-trees, *ACM Transactions on Database Systems*, 6(1):174-193, 1981.
16. Roussopoulos, N. and Leifker, D., Direct Spatial Search on Pictorial Database Using Packed R-trees, *ACM International Conference on Management of Data,* pages 17-31, 1985.
17. Ruemmler, C. and Wilkes, J., An Introduction to Disk Drive Modeling, *IEEE Computer*, March 1994.
18. White, D.A., & Jain, R. (1996). Similarity Indexing with the SS-tree. *Proc. 12th IEEE Conf. on Data Engineering* (pp. 516-523).

Author Index

Lecture Notes in Computer Science

For information about Vols. 1–3803

please contact your bookseller or Springer

Vol. 3847: K.P. Jantke, A. Lunzer, N. Spyratos, Y. Tanaka (Eds.), Federation over the Web. X, 215 pages. 2006. (Sublibrary LNAI).

Vol. 3846: H. J. van den Herik, Y. Björnsson, N.S. Netanyahu (Eds.), Computers and Games. XIV, 333 pages. 2006.

Vol. 3845: J. Farré, I. Litovsky, S. Schmitz (Eds.), Implementation and Application of Automata. XIII, 360 pages. 2006.

Vol. 3844: J.-M. Bruel (Ed.), Satellite Events at the MoDELS 2005 Conference. XIII, 360 pages. 2006.

Vol. 3843: P. Healy, N.S. Nikolov (Eds.), Graph Drawing. XVII, 536 pages. 2006.

Vol. 3842: H.T. Shen, J. Li, M. Li, J. Ni, W. Wang (Eds.), Advanced Web and Network Technologies, and Applications. XXVII, 1057 pages. 2006.

Vol. 3841: X. Zhou, J. Li, H.T. Shen, M. Kitsuregawa, Y. Zhang (Eds.), Frontiers of WWW Research and Development - APWeb 2006. XXIV, 1223 pages. 2006.

Vol. 3840: M. Li, B. Boehm, L.J. Osterweil (Eds.), Unifying the Software Process Spectrum. XVI, 522 pages. 2006.

Vol. 3839: J.-C. Filliâtre, C. Paulin-Mohring, B. Werner (Eds.), Types for Proofs and Programs. VIII, 275 pages. 2006.

Vol. 3838: A. Middeldorp, V. van Oostrom, F. van Raamsdonk, R. de Vrijer (Eds.), Processes, Terms and Cycles: Steps on the Road to Infinity. XVIII, 639 pages. 2005.

Vol. 3837: K. Cho, P. Jacquet (Eds.), Technologies for Advanced Heterogeneous Networks. IX, 307 pages. 2005.

Vol. 3836: J.-M. Pierson (Ed.), Data Management in Grids. X, 143 pages. 2006.

Vol. 3835: G. Sutcliffe, A. Voronkov (Eds.), Logic for Programming, Artificial Intelligence, and Reasoning. XIV, 744 pages. 2005. (Sublibrary LNAI).

Vol. 3834: D.G. Feitelson, E. Frachtenberg, L. Rudolph, U. Schwiegelshohn (Eds.), Job Scheduling Strategies for Parallel Processing. VIII, 283 pages. 2005.

Vol. 3833: K.-J. Li, C. Vangenot (Eds.), Web and Wireless Geographical Information Systems. XI, 309 pages. 2005.

Vol. 3832: D. Zhang, A.K. Jain (Eds.), Advances in Biometrics. XX, 796 pages. 2005.

Vol. 3831: J. Wiedermann, G. Tel, J. Pokorný, M. Bieliková, J. Štuller (Eds.), SOFSEM 2006: Theory and Practice of Computer Science. XV, 576 pages. 2006.

Vol. 3830: D. Weyns, H. V.D. Parunak, F. Michel (Eds.), Environments for Multi-Agent Systems II. VIII, 291 pages. 2006. (Sublibrary LNAI).

Vol. 3829: P. Pettersson, W. Yi (Eds.), Formal Modeling and Analysis of Timed Systems. IX, 305 pages. 2005.

Vol. 3828: X. Deng, Y. Ye (Eds.), Internet and Network Economics. XVII, 1106 pages. 2005.

Vol. 3827: X. Deng, D.-Z. Du (Eds.), Algorithms and Computation. XX, 1190 pages. 2005.

Vol. 3826: B. Benatallah, F. Casati, P. Traverso (Eds.), Service-Oriented Computing - ICSOC 2005. XVIII, 597 pages. 2005.

Vol. 3824: L.T. Yang, M. Amamiya, Z. Liu, M. Guo, F.J. Rammig (Eds.), Embedded and Ubiquitous Computing – EUC 2005. XXIII, 1204 pages. 2005.

Vol. 3823: T. Enokido, L. Yan, B. Xiao, D. Kim, Y. Dai, L.T. Yang (Eds.), Embedded and Ubiquitous Computing – EUC 2005 Workshops. XXXII, 1317 pages. 2005.

Vol. 3822: D. Feng, D. Lin, M. Yung (Eds.), Information Security and Cryptology. XII, 420 pages. 2005.

Vol. 3821: R. Ramanujam, S. Sen (Eds.), FSTTCS 2005: Foundations of Software Technology and Theoretical Computer Science. XIV, 566 pages. 2005.

Vol. 3820: L.T. Yang, X.-s. Zhou, W. Zhao, Z. Wu, Y. Zhu, M. Lin (Eds.), Embedded Software and Systems. XXVIII, 779 pages. 2005.

Vol. 3819: P. Van Hentenryck (Ed.), Practical Aspects of Declarative Languages. X, 231 pages. 2005.

Vol. 3818: S. Grumbach, L. Sui, V. Vianu (Eds.), Advances in Computer Science – ASIAN 2005. XIII, 294 pages. 2005.

Vol. 3817: M. Faundez-Zanuy, L. Janer, A. Esposito, A. Satue-Villar, J. Roure, V. Espinosa-Duro (Eds.), Nonlinear Analyses and Algorithms for Speech Processing. XII, 380 pages. 2006. (Sublibrary LNAI).

Vol. 3816: G. Chakraborty (Ed.), Distributed Computing and Internet Technology. XXI, 606 pages. 2005.

Vol. 3815: E.A. Fox, E.J. Neuhold, P. Premsmit, V. Wuwongse (Eds.), Digital Libraries: Implementing Strategies and Sharing Experiences. XVII, 529 pages. 2005.

Vol. 3814: M. Maybury, O. Stock, W. Wahlster (Eds.), Intelligent Technologies for Interactive Entertainment. XV, 342 pages. 2005. (Sublibrary LNAI).

Vol. 3813: R. Molva, G. Tsudik, D. Westhoff (Eds.), Security and Privacy in Ad-hoc and Sensor Networks. VIII, 219 pages. 2005.

Vol. 3812: C. Bussler, A. Haller (Eds.), Business Process Management Workshops. XIII, 520 pages. 2006.

Vol. 3811: C. Bussler, M.-C. Shan (Eds.), Technologies for E-Services. VIII, 127 pages. 2006.

Vol. 3810: Y.G. Desmedt, H. Wang, Y. Mu, Y. Li (Eds.), Cryptology and Network Security. XI, 349 pages. 2005.

Vol. 3809: S. Zhang, R. Jarvis (Eds.), AI 2005: Advances in Artificial Intelligence. XXVII, 1344 pages. 2005. (Sublibrary LNAI).

Vol. 3808: C. Bento, A. Cardoso, G. Dias (Eds.), Progress in Artificial Intelligence. XVIII, 704 pages. 2005. (Sublibrary LNAI).

Vol. 3807: M. Dean, Y. Guo, W. Jun, R. Kaschek, S. Krishnaswamy, Z. Pan, Q.Z. Sheng (Eds.), Web Information Systems Engineering – WISE 2005 Workshops. XV, 275 pages. 2005.

Vol. 3806: A.H. H. Ngu, M. Kitsuregawa, E.J. Neuhold, J.-Y. Chung, Q.Z. Sheng (Eds.), Web Information Systems Engineering – WISE 2005. XXI, 771 pages. 2005.

Vol. 3805: G. Subsol (Ed.), Virtual Storytelling. XII, 289 pages. 2005.

Vol. 3804: G. Bebis, R. Boyle, D. Koracin, B. Parvin (Eds.), Advances in Visual Computing. XX, 755 pages. 2005.